Praise for *Small Groups for the Rest of Us*

In *Small Groups For The Rest of Us*, Chris gives practical, proven ideas for building a small-groups system that goes beyond the typical church attender. This book is for all leaders trying to make small groups work inside and outside their churches.

—JUD WILHITE, AUTHOR OF *PURSUED*,
SR. PASTOR CENTRAL CHRISTIAN CHURCH

Chris Surratt led the very first small group we joined when we moved to Nashville, and it was awesome. I'm so happy he's sharing his years of wisdom with the rest of the world because small groups are critical to building real community in churches, and he's an expert!

—JON ACUFF - *NEW YORK TIMES* BEST-
SELLING AUTHOR OF *DO OVER*, *START* AND
STUFF CHRISTIANS LIKE

I am so thrilled Chris Surratt has put his ideas and many years of ministry and group experience down on paper. *Small Groups for the Rest of Us* is a thoughtful and helpful book for any ministry leader, but especially for those of us in the trenches leading the small-group initiative at our churches. Each chapter is chocked full of wisdom with helpful insights on how to create an intentional and thriving small-group mini... *Fringes*, is worth the entire price of the book... implement it fully. It's that good.

—BILL WILLI...
MINISTRY ENV...
MINISTRIES, CO-AUTHOR OF *CREATING*
COMMUNITY

As I read this book, I kept thinking over and over again, "Man! I wish I'd written this book!" And "Man! I wish I'd had this book thirty years ago!" *Small Groups For The Rest of Us* is a book not just for "the rest of us," but for *all* of us. At Saddleback, we say that a healthy small group is one that seeks to fulfill the Great Commission and the Great Commandment. We equip them to develop health by balancing the five biblical purposes. This book, in their hands, *will help make their group healthier*. It doesn't matter what system of groups you are trying to work, or whether you have a system at all. This book will challenge how you think, who you reach, and the power of biblical community to change lives. You'll laugh, you'll cry, and you'll get out of your comfortable chair to reach people nobody else is reaching . . . people Jesus loves. People just like you and me. People who are way different than you and me. People who desperately need life-giving relationships, just like you and me.

—STEVE GLADEN, PASTOR OF THE SMALL
GROUP COMMUNITY, SADDLEBACK CHURCH
AUTHOR, *SMALL GROUPS WITH PURPOSE &*
LEADING SMALL GROUPS WITH PURPOSE

You won't just read this; instead, you'll feel as if you're shadowing Chris as he navigates every strategic decision required for building transformational groups in a church. Loaded with ground-level wisdom that is refreshingly vulnerable, brutally honest, intensely practical, and readily transferable to your group ministry.

—DR. BILL DONAHUE, AUTHOR OF
THE IRRESISTIBLE COMMUNITY: AN
INVITATION TO LIFE TOGETHER

When a groups pastor tells you that 90 percent of their adult membership is in a small group, you can rest assured that person knows how to connect every type of person to a small group. If you want to do the same, buy this book, read this book, and make this book your handbook so you can, "present *every* person mature in Christ" (Colossians 1:28 NET).

—RICK HOWERTON, DISCIPLESHIP AND
SMALL GROUP SPECIALIST, LIFEWAY
CHURCH RESOURCES

We have over promised and under delivered on our claims for life in groups and community for far too long. In *Small Groups for the Rest of Us* Chris Surratt slaughters some of our sacred cows, challenges our perspectives, and offers new ideas for helping people discover, engage, and enjoy life together. He brings valuable experience from years in the trenches and offers practical ideas for ensuring groups are accessible to a wider range of people in your church and community. I've been learning from Chris for years, and I'm excited to share this resource with our team!

—HEATHER ZEMPEL, DISCIPLESHIP
PASTOR, NATIONAL COMMUNITY CHURCH
AUTHOR OF *AMAZED AND CONFUSED*,
COMMUNITY IS MESSY & SACRED ROADS

SMALL GROUPS

GROUPS

—— *for* ——

THE REST OF US

Chris
Surratt

NE☒T
LEADERSHIP NETWORK

SMALL
GROUPS
— *for* —
THE REST
OF US

how to design
your small-
groups system
to reach the
fringes

THOMAS NELSON
Since 1798

Published in Nashville, Tennessee, by Thomas Nelson. Thomas Nelson is a registered trademark of Thomas Nelson, Inc.

Thomas Nelson, Inc., titles may be purchased in bulk for educational, business, fund-raising, or sales promotional use. For information, please e-mail *SpecialMarkets@ThomasNelson.com*.

Unless otherwise noted, all Scripture quotations are taken from the New Century Version®. Copyright © 1987, 1988, 1991 by Thomas Nelson, Inc. All rights reserved.

Scriptures marked NIV are taken from the HOLY BIBLE: NEW INTERNATIONAL VERSION®. © 1973, 1978, 1984 by International Bible Society. Used by permission of Zondervan Publishing House. All rights reserved.

Library of Congress Control Number: 2014959021

Softcover: 978-0718-0323-1-9
e-Book: 978-0718-0323-2-6

Printed in the United States of America

15 16 17 18 19 20 RRD 6 5 4 3 2 1

To all of the small group hosts and leaders who make time every single week to clean your homes, prepare cheese trays, and invite groups of people over to discover Jesus in a new way. You are my heroes.

About Leadership ✖ Network

Leadership Network fosters innovation movements that activate the church to greater impact. We help shape the conversations and practices of pacesetter churches in North America and around the world. The Leadership Network mind-set identifies church leaders with forward-thinking ideas—and helps them to catalyze those ideas resulting in movements that shape the church.

Together with HarperCollins Christian Publishing, the biggest name in Christian books, the NEXT imprint of Leadership Network moves ideas to implementation for leaders to take their ideas to form, substance, and reality. Placed in the hands of other church leaders, that reality begins spreading from one leader to the next . . . and to the next . . . and to the next, where that idea begins to flourish into a full-grown movement that creates a real, tangible impact in the world around it.

NEXT: A Leadership Network Resource
committed to helping you grow your next idea.

leadnet.org/NEXT

Contents

Foreword

I will never forget cramming about ten guys into my college dorm room at Western Kentucky University. Our college pastor, Rick Howerton, had challenged my roommate and me to get a group of friends together and start a small group. It sounded like a great idea . . . until there I sat in a circle with these ten guys looking back at me with blank stares, clearly wondering, "So, what now?"

I'll never forget just how ill equipped I felt to lead that group.

Well, amazingly enough, almost two decades later I still lead a small group. Almost every week a group of adults gather in our living room to laugh, cry, study, and share life together. I feel a lot more comfortable these days, but I still have my moments of anxiety, uncertainty, and even (if I'm really honest) dread. That's why I've been eager to get my hands on this book. I think all of us who lead a group or groups ministry know that ministry in the small-group setting is important, essential, and working. I also think we believe just as strongly that something is often missing, it could be better, and we need help to take things to the next level.

I'm so excited that Chris Surratt has taken the time to sit down and put his small-group wisdom into book form for all of us to devour. Chris is a person of steadfast devotion to Christ and persistent enthusiasm for being a pastor. I'm so thankful Chris has helped us navigate the challenges of putting together a life-changing community-groups ministry here at Cross Point. I've seen firsthand the difference the principles and ideas in this book can make in a church. Hundreds of lives have been impacted because of his diligence in this area of ministry, and now I'm sure your ministry will be impacted by it as well.

Out of the depths of his involvement and experience, Chris has written an exceptional book for any church leader. Whether you're thinking of transitioning to small groups or have been doing them for years, you'll find this resource extremely helpful. This is the kind of book anyone who has led or is considering leading a group should read as Chris helps us through so many of the practical challenges we all face doing small-group ministry. It's my prayer that churches will use this book as a practical guide for engaging people in community so we can all fulfill our God-given kingdom mission. I know small-group ministry can sometimes be a challenge. But it's a challenge worth taking on.

I'm genuinely excited for you as you begin your journey through the pages of this book. Your beliefs will be challenged, your spirit encouraged, and your faith stirred.

Pete Wilson

Acknowledgments

This book would not have been possible if not for the support of many people along the way. I am useless without my community.

To my pastor and friend, Pete Wilson: You have allowed us to dream about what the possibilities are and then backed us as we chased after them. Thank you for your never-wavering vision of a church that goes and loves.

To the Cross Point Groups team: You guys inspire me every day with your passion to see people connected in biblical communities. Thank you for sharing your stories with me.

To my brother, Geoff, who has walked alongside me throughout the whole writing process: This book would have never been finished without your ideas, counsel, and sarcastic texts.

To my family, Greg and Dee: Greg, thank you for allowing me to be a small part of the amazing story of Seacoast Church. Your leadership helped shape who I am today. Dee, thank you for being my second mom growing up!

To my dad, Hubert Surratt, who gave me my first shot in ministry as an extremely naive, inexperienced student pastor.

To my small group: You guys have walked with us through everything imaginable over the past five years. Thank you for really knowing me and still showing up every Tuesday night at our house!

To my small-group world friends: Rick Howerton, Ben Reed, Steve Gladen, Eddie Mosley, Bill Donahue, Mark Howell, and countless others. Thank you for accepting me into the tribe.

To Greg Ligon, Mark Sweeney, and the entire Leadership Network team: I never would have dreamed that a casual conversation in the lobby at the Catalyst Conference would lead to a book! Thank you for believing in my ideas and allowing me to be a part of this new venture with Harper Collins.

To the team at Thomas Nelson: LeeEric Fesco, David Moberg, and many others. Thank you for your support and guidance through this journey. You have helped make this a great experience!

And most of all, to my family: Jenny, Brianna, and Ashlyn. You guys are my foundation and the reason why I look forward to every day. Jenny, thank you for following me around the country on this crazy journey for the last twenty-two years. The way you love people unconditionally inspires me to be a better person. Brianna and Ashlyn, I am so proud to be your daddy! Keep chasing after God and your dreams with everything you have.

Introduction

By almost every measurement you can think of I am the last person who should be writing a book about small groups in the church.

- I am an introvert. The small-group world is naturally built for the extroverted people who build energy from being around other extroverts. I get reenergized only after I have been with people and can finally decompress through a good book or quiet time with my family. Sad fact about me: I dread our weekly small-group meeting all day every week. I am *always* thankful for our group after the meeting, but the thought of getting my energy level up for it every week wears me out.
- I am late to the game. I have been a part of churches with small groups for many years, but I have only been able to completely focus on groups for the past five years. I quickly realized everything that I don't know about small groups after coming to Cross Point Church in 2009. I am so thankful for those who have gone before me and written books to tell their story. I read all of them in the first two years after moving to Nashville. I am also thankful for the

networks of small-group Point people that I have been graciously invited to be a part of. They have allowed me to do a lot of listening and not too much talking as I soak in their years of experience and knowledge.

- I am not a hugger. For whatever reason, the small-group world puts a high priority on the act of hugging another person. I come from a long line of nonhuggers in my family, so my adverseness to bodily contact is a very natural reaction. This is especially difficult when you grow up in the South, where everyone hugs everyone for any reason. My native Texan wife is completely the opposite of me. She grew up in a family where leaving the room for a few minutes to use the restroom was as good an excuse as any to dole out a few hugs. If you run into me in the church lobby, I will accept a hug but probably not initiate it.

As I have begun to immerse myself in everything small groups over the last few years, I have discovered there are a lot more people like me who are currently sitting on the outside of community because they don't fit into our small-group boxes. We have designed systems to reach people who are already being reached. Most of the people in our small groups would have found community somewhere else if we didn't offer it through the church. But what about the outliers who are privately yearning for someone else to walk alongside them on their journey but cannot find anything for themselves in our systems?

The reasons why I should not be writing a book about small groups have become the focus of my life: everyone needs community, and we have to make it easy for them to find it. Research has repeatedly shown that being part of a community is critical for our well-being. The following comes from a study I found at PBS.org about connection and happiness:

> Researchers have found that people are happier when they are with other people than when they are alone—and the "boost" is the same for introverts and extroverts. They also are finding that happy people are more pleasant, helpful, and sociable. So being around people makes us feel happier, and when we are happier we are more fun to be around, creating an "upward spiral" of happiness.[1]

So even we introverts are more fun to be around when we are in community together! In order to offer biblical community to the rest of us, we have to start expanding the possibilities of what small groups could be. This will be a stretch for some. The way it's been is comfortable. It's safe. But the landscape is shifting around us, and the church is being left behind. It will take different ideas and ways of thinking to ultimately reach the unreached with community.

This book is not designed to be a how-to for doing small groups in your church. There are some practical suggestions and a few ideas that have worked (and not worked) for us, but they are here to be thought starters. There is no small-group system that will function the same in every church. A perfect system does not exist.

My goal with this book is to give you permission to take a fresh look at whom you are currently targeting for your groups. Take what could work for your church and make it better. Even if you disagree with my ideas, they will at least cause you to reexamine why you do what you're doing. We small-group people have the most important job in the church: we are responsible for providing environments for people to grow spiritually and have fun while doing it. No one in or out of our churches should have to miss out on it.

And I will be looking for a hug the next time I see you.

Small Groups Are Weird

We are all a little weird. And we like to think that
there is always someone weirder. I mean, I am sure
some of you are looking at me and thinking, "Well,
at least I am not as weird as you," and I am thinking,
"Well, at least I am not as weird as the people in
the loony bin," and the people in the loony bin
are thinking, "Well, at least I am an orange."
—Jim Gaffigan, *Dad Is Fat*

Let's go ahead and get this out of the way from the beginning: to the
normal church outsider, small groups are weird. Those of us who are
tasked with convincing people in our churches that joining a small
group is something they should do have an uphill battle. Here are just

a few of the perceptions that come along with signing up for a small group in a church:

- Carve out two to three hours a week from your already impossible schedule.
- Spend those two to three hours with strangers in someone's home.
- Be prepared to confess all of your internal struggles to those strangers.
- Don't forget to stop by the store every week to pick up a cheese-and-fruit tray for the group.

Sound like fun? It didn't to me. My journey to being a small-groups pastor was not an easy one. In fact, I pretty much came to it kicking and screaming.

My Journey to Groups

I will never forget my first experience at an early morning men's breakfast. I will admit that I am not by nature an early morning person. At that point in my life (early twenties and a musician), I had no clue there were two five o'clocks in the day. So I was not in the best frame of mind when I walked into the back room of the restaurant at 5:30 a.m. for the breakfast.

Everything about the meeting was great until it came time for the small-group discussion with the guys sitting around my table. The assignment was for each of us to confess to the table our biggest current struggle in our walk with God and then spend a few minutes praying for one another to overcome the sin. I had never met any of the men at my table, so there was no chance I was going to open the vaults to my deepest, darkest struggles. Instead, I silently prayed that no one would look at me to go first. We started going around the table, and it quickly became evident that a couple of the guys did not have the same inner boundaries that I did. They were confessing sins I am pretty certain were illegal in a couple of states. By the time it was my turn to speak, the confession bar had been set pretty high. I could feel disapproving stares burning through me as I looked down at my plate and muttered something about not reading my Bible and praying enough. You know, the adult equivalent of when I ask my kids what they learned in their class at church and they answer, "Jesus." We finished the confessions, and I quickly left the restaurant, pretty certain that I did not want to have anything to do with any future men's small groups.

Fast-forward twenty years and discover that I am now such a big believer in the power of community through small groups that I lead a groups ministry at a church that has over 90 percent of our adult members attending a group somewhere in our city.

Did a few men's group experiences get less awkward? Nope.

Did people's lives get less messy? Nope.

What happened is very simple: I discovered the power of real life change when I dropped the facade of being a Sunday Christian and began to live the raw truth of life with people as messed up as I am.

Until I decided to become vulnerable with a group of people I trusted, I thought I was the only one:

The only one who sometimes questioned if God was real. (I am a pastor.)

The only one who didn't always feel like reading my Bible
and praying. (Did I mention I am a pastor?)
The only one who dropped the ball with my family.
The only one who started with a smile on Sunday morning
and finished with anger on Sunday night.

C. S. Lewis defined friendship this way: "The typical expression
of opening Friendship would be something like, 'What? You too? I
thought I was the only one.'"[1]

That is the secret sauce of a small group. When we help create
environments where messed-up people like us are able to look at
each other and say, "You too?" it frames the message of the gospel
in a whole new way. Suddenly people understand grace in a context
they never knew before. It doesn't matter what the circumstances are
that brought them to this place. It only matters that someone else
understands.

The journey from attending to leading small groups has not
always felt like a successful one. After being on staff at Seacoast
Church in Charleston, South Carolina, for ten years, my family and
I moved to Greenville to launch a campus for Seacoast in the upstate
area. I knew the best way to build community for a new church was to
start small groups as soon as possible. So we did. We had purposefully
picked our new home based on how easy it would be to host a large
number of people. The kitchen was spacious for prediscussion time,
and the living room had plenty of room to arrange chairs around the
outside. We had as many as forty-four people crammed into our house
at one time.

Our philosophy of leading groups at the time was to lead a group for a semester and then hand it off to an apprentice leader while we started a new group. Our first couple of groups averaged ten to fifteen couples, so we felt confident that the system was working and we were starting to figure out this small-groups thing. That was true—right up until we opened the sign-up sheet for the third semester and only one couple committed to our group. Even though we continued to invite (or beg) other people to join, our small group stayed truly small the entire semester. It was never a difficult decision whether to cancel a group meeting or not. When the other couple couldn't make it to group night, it was canceled. So much for my perfect record as a successful small-group leader.

Even though not every group we led through the years has felt like a home run, I will forever champion small groups with everything I have. I know they are difficult and far from perfect, but so is my life. I have come to the realization that the sole reason my small group is weird is because I am in it. I wouldn't have it any other way.

Small-Group Models

In my twenty-two years of church-staff life I have run across almost every type of small-group model you can think of. The first version was a Sunday school system in my dad's Pentecostal church in Houston, Texas, which had a predominately lecture format in which different age groups met for an hour before the church service for focused Bible study. All of our Sunday school classes were held at the church, and people graduated level by level until eventually they landed in the senior adult class that met in the auditorium.

The first time my wife and I experienced small groups that met outside of the church building was when we moved to Charleston in 1995 to go on staff at Seacoast Church. Seacoast is a nondenominational church started in 1988 by my brother, Greg Surratt. At that time, all of Seacoast's small groups met on Friday nights in homes across the city, with shared babysitting offered at the church. The meetings were mostly Bible studies, with a few groups digging deeper into the message from the previous Sunday.

After a few years we heard about a discipleship movement that was sweeping parts of the world based on the idea of circles of twelve. The concept was that your church would break into circles of twelve, and a leader was selected to lead one circle, mentor another circle, and belong to a third circle. This system required a minimum of three meetings a week and a whole bunch of interlocking circles on whiteboards. It may have worked beautifully in South America, but it didn't last long in South Carolina.

Ted Haggard's book *Dog Training, Fly Fishing, and Sharing Christ in the 21st Century*[2] introduced us to the concept of free-market small groups. The basic concept was that small groups have common interests (such as training dogs, fly fishing, etc.). This system allows people to build community around something they are already doing. Versions of the free-market system can be found in churches across the nation today: running groups, fishing groups, softball groups, water-skiing groups, golfing groups, new moms groups, underwater basket-weaving groups (not really underwater basket-weaving, but you get my point). A free-market system is great for assimilating a lot of people into small groups; however, you have to make sure those groups include God. Otherwise they're just social clubs with a theme.

Groups at Cross Point

The foundation for community groups at Cross Point is based on the vision for the overall church: to be a community of believers radically devoted to Christ, irrevocably committed to one another, and relentlessly dedicated to reaching those outside God's family with the gospel of Christ. Each group is expected to pursue all three things: discipleship, community, and evangelism. We see this being modeled for us by the small groups in the early church.

> They spent their time learning the apostles' teaching, sharing, breaking bread, and praying together.
> The apostles were doing many miracles and signs, and everyone felt great respect for God. All the believers were together and shared everything. They would sell their land and the things they owned and then divide the money and give it to anyone who needed it. The believers met together in the Temple every day. They ate together in their homes, happy to share their food with joyful hearts. They praised God and were liked by all the people. Every day the Lord added those who were being saved to the group of believers. (Acts 2:42–47)

1. Discipleship: Radically Devoted to Christ

It's clear in this passage that the early church spent time not only learning from the apostle's teachings but also living it out together.

Our group leaders at Cross Point are asked to simply be one step ahead of those they lead in their journey to be more like Christ, and they should be willing to take someone else along with them. We recognize that discipleship is not a cookie-cutter process. Each person will grow differently and at a different pace than everyone else. The key is to help them identify where they are and what it will take to help them get to the next step. We will dive into this in another chapter, but discipleship is not easy and it's not fast.

2. Community: Irrevocably Committed to One Another

The groups in the early church "ate together in their homes, happy to share their food with joyful hearts." Community is not a difficult value for Cross Point's groups to implement, because it starts with our senior pastor, Pete Wilson. If you attend a Sunday morning service at our Nashville campus (the campus where Pete speaks), you will likely find Pete between services hugging and talking to people in the lobby. At some point someone will have to drag him to the stage for the message. Even though there are thousands of people who now attend on a weekly basis, Pete still takes time to talk to anyone who wants to talk to him.

You will also find worship leaders and band members greeting people at the doors or, on a rainy Sunday, running into the parking lot to walk someone in with an umbrella. There is no green room hiding at Cross Point.

A new church member, who had been attending for a couple of months, asked me during a lunch, "How do you guys create community as a church? As soon as you walk in the doors you feel it!"

The answer starts with leadership. Pete models and the church follows. This translates all the way through our community group leaders.

Community is essential, but it's easy to stay there and not move on to number three.

3. Evangelism: Relentlessly Dedicated to Reaching Those Outside

From the passage in Acts it's obvious that evangelism was essential to the early church groups: "Every day the Lord added those who were being saved to the group of believers." Of the three building blocks for groups, evangelism is the most difficult one to continue practicing. It's easy for groups to slip into the "us four and no more" mentality. As soon as a group becomes inward focused, it becomes a holy huddle and not the Great Commission. At Cross Point, we train our leaders to look at the example Jesus gave us. Jesus had his small group of twelve, but discipleship was accomplished through the mission. They were consistently taking the words of Jesus and putting them into practice. James 1:22 says, "Do what God's teaching says; when you only listen and do nothing, you are fooling yourselves." Our group leaders need to know that the curriculum is important, but it's worthless without living it out.

Groups Are the Option

Because we believe sustained life change happens best in the context of community, we make small groups the priority option for spiritual growth in our church. Many churches offer a variety of classes for people to choose from to help them grow in biblical knowledge. While I don't believe there is anything fundamentally wrong with offering classes, we see the group-learning format as the best direction for our church. Here are a few reasons why it works for us:

1. *Offsite groups solve space problems.* As a growing, multisite church, on-campus space will always be an issue for us. Even if we wanted to offer a more traditional Sunday school format for classes, we would not have anywhere to put them. A few of our campuses are portable, and they are allowed to use just enough rooms to pull off a Sunday morning experience with worship and kids. Even our permanent facilities are completely packed on Sundays with what it takes to create an effective environment for families. We could build more buildings and continue adding rooms, but there will never be enough space. Small groups in homes all over the city are the best answer to space problems for us.

2. *Small groups provide accountability.* The only way to continue growing spiritually is through honest accountability with another person. Proverbs 27:17 says, "As iron sharpens iron, so people can improve each other." This level of sharpening happens best in a small-group setting with other believers.

3. *Small groups limit choices.* It seems reasonable that the more options we have, the better, but the opposite is, in fact, true. Recent studies show that people are paralyzed when they have too many choices. One of my favorite restaurants in the world is In-N-Out Burger. They offer four things on their menu: hamburgers, cheeseburgers, shakes, and drinks. That's it. It helps that their burgers are really, really good, but I love that

I don't have to think about it when I go in. I just order a cheese-burger and fries. I also love the food at the Cheesecake Factory, but the twenty-page menu of options frustrates me. Apple recognized this early on and created products that are simple and obvious. One button is all you need. When new people visit our church and ask us what they should do next, there's only one button: join a small group. If small groups are just an option on a long menu of choices, they will lose every time.

4. *Small groups broaden the span of pastoral care.* We could never hire enough staff to facilitate spiritual care for every person who attends our church. Starting a small group gives people opportunities to discover their God-given gifts and abilities through leading. Instead of hiring more staff pastors to keep up with the growth, we have commissioned 250 leaders to pastor their small circles of community. Our group leaders are the first line of care in the church. If one of our pastors is required to make a hospital visit because of an emergency, the person's small group is almost always already waiting there.

5. *Small groups create a natural pipeline for leadership.* Most churches are asking, "Where do you find leaders?" A small-group system is an ideal incubator for potential leaders and future staff members. If you want to find out if people will follow someone, ask them to start a small group. If you want to find out if someone can build teams, ask them to coach three to five small-group leaders for a semester. Looking for your next campus pastor? Look for the small-group leader you keep encouraging to start new groups because their own group has grown to the size of a small church.

6. *Small groups make a large church feel small.* We all want our churches to grow, but the downside to growth is the loss of personal intimacy. After the church grows beyond three hundred people, it's impossible for attendees to know everyone. This is exasperated when a church turns to multiple services, and it is completely lost when a church becomes multisite. The only way to keep people from falling through the cracks is by creating a system to catch them. Small groups help the church keep people who would otherwise drift back into anonymity. We all long for the feeling that someone knows our name on Sunday morning. Small groups provide it.

7. *Small groups reinforce the message.* More than 75 percent of our groups at Cross Point use our message studies for their weekly curriculum. Because of that number, we are very intentional about what we put in their hands each week. We currently partner with an outside organization to turn message manuscripts into a comprehensive study for our groups to use. The studies include additional scriptures and commentary to take the message a little deeper. We also provide a one-page version for our hosts and leaders who prefer fewer options. Any senior pastor would be thrilled to know that people are talking about their Sunday message throughout the week.

8. *Small groups identify the core.* When we are looking for where we should plant our next campus at Cross Point, the first information we access is how many small groups are in that area. When we need to quickly respond to a need or a natural disaster, our first line of action is our group leaders. We saw the power of this during the 2010 Nashville flood. Hundreds

of homes and businesses were destroyed overnight by over nineteen inches of nonstop rain. Amid the devastation we watched small groups instinctively pull together and be the Acts 2:45 church. People opened their homes for group members who had lost everything. It took some people months to get back on their feet, but their small groups never wavered in support. Church membership is no longer the core of a church; small groups are.

9. *Small groups are easily replicable.* As your church begins to grow, you have to decide what will expand. Excellent classes are difficult to pull off across multiple locations. Large-group gatherings become less viable with space at a premium. Staple ministries (men's, women's, seniors', etc.) are quickly maxed out or marginalized with a lack of staff to pour their time and focus into them. The one ministry that has no limits is small groups. You are only limited by the number of homes, businesses, and apartment clubhouses in your city. Instead of attempting to start another men's ministry, kick off a few men's small groups. Thinking about launching a new campus? Start with a monthly gathering of three to four small groups in that area. Small groups are limitless when it comes to a church's reach in a city.

The Best-Laid Plans

Despite all of the benefits small groups can bring to a church, providing biblical community for everyone is hard work. Just like the people in the groups are messy, even the most thought-out groups system can go sideways at times. The best approach to building a lasting groups system is to plan for flexibility. An open mind-set will allow group leaders to follow where God is moving in the church, and not just in the circles and lines on our whiteboards.

When I came to Cross Point in 2009, the small groups system was organic. There was not a lot of formal training for leaders, and the overall structure was pretty loose. When we did a snapshot survey of how many people were actually attending groups, we discovered that only 33 percent of our adults said they were actively involved in a group on a weekly basis. That was a long way from our stated goal of at least 80 percent in groups. We spent the next four years implementing new systems and training to make it easier for new people to get connected within new groups. For our most recent semester, we have around 92 percent of our adult attendance participating in groups. It was a *huge* win for our all-star team of mostly volunteer groups staff, but it wasn't easy.

As a systems guy, I love coming up with new ways to achieve a goal. To paraphrase John "Hannibal" Smith from *The A Team*: "I love it when a good system comes together."[3] There's something about putting a plan down on a whiteboard and then seeing it come to life when implemented well by inspired leaders. Fortunately for all of us, whiteboards are designed to erase and start over. Over the last four years we have tweaked and started over many times with our groups systems.

- My first attempt at implementing a functional coaching system completely failed.
- We reshot our first training videos three times before they were good enough to use.
- We discovered early on that after a compelling message on why community matters by our senior pastor, people will

sign up in droves on Sunday morning, but a lot of them will not show up for group later that week.

- Our first attempt at a connection event was a disaster.
- Despite implementing several layers of redundancy in our communications system, people still occasionally are not contacted when they sign up for a group.
- We are on our third different groups database in three years.
- We still do not have a great system for measuring spiritual health in our groups.

It's conceivable that we will reach a 90 percent participation level in our groups, but not without a ton of hustle and mistakes along the way. And with everything we have accomplished in the last four years, there is still a long way to go. We will continue to tweak and start over as many times as we need to until every person in our circle of influence is being discipled within a growing biblical community.

Think It Over

- What is the driving vision for groups in your church?
- What group models have you seen work best in churches?
- How many options do you currently offer attendees for spiritual growth? Are any of those pulling people away from being in small groups?
- List the potential benefits of small groups for your church.
- What is your current groups system? Is it time to be changed or tweaked to be more effective?

Reaching the Fringes

We with our lives are like islands in the sea, or
like trees in the forest. The maple and the pine
may whisper to each other with their leaves. . . .
But the trees also commingle their roots in the
darkness underground, and the islands also
hang together through the ocean's bottom.
—William James, "Confidences of a
'Psychical Researcher'" (1909)

From day one, the vision for small groups at Cross Point has always
been to have at least 80 percent of our adult attenders participate.
That is a daunting number for the staff charged with the mission, but
we have held tight to the idea that sustained life change happens best

in the context of community. Coming to church for an hour every Sunday is not enough to change the world. We were designed by God to walk this life shoulder to shoulder with other people.

If we truly believe everyone should be in groups, we have to start thinking beyond typical church members who brave our connection systems to eventually sit in a stranger's living room. There are people on the fringes of our churches not currently being invited into community. Some of these people will make us uncomfortable. They will challenge our small-group leaders. They will evoke strongly worded e-mails from other church members to the pastoral staff. But they will never be reached if we continue to pretend they don't exist. To paraphrase Apple's 1997 advertising slogan, it's time to start thinking differently.

Reaching Introverts

*How many introverts does it take
to change a lightbulb?
Why does it have to be a group activity?!*

I will never forget the night I stood onstage in the gym where we were hosting our first-ever connection event at Cross Point. A connection event is basically speed dating for small groups. People came to experience what a group was like in a neutral setting before committing to show up at someone's house for six weeks. We set up round tables across the gym where different types of groups would be represented with leaders and hosts sitting at each table. A person could visit and talk to the leaders before choosing a table to sit at and begin community.

This was our first event, so we planned for around two hundred to three hundred people to show up. And that number was stretching the capacity of the small gymnasium in the Baptist church we leased for our Nashville campus. Our team was excited to see this strategy put into action after months and months of planning.

It was complete chaos.

Instead of the two hundred to three hundred people we were expecting, more than four hundred eventually squeezed down the narrow stairs from the auditorium to the gym. We quit counting once panic set in. As I stood onstage, ready to start the event, I saw a quiet, reserved woman burst into tears in the middle of the room and make a Carl Lewis–worthy sprint to the door, probably to never give small groups another chance.

In that moment I knew we were going to have to come up with alternative on-ramps to groups than this massive extroverted-friendly approach. There were hundreds of people we were missing by taking a "one size fits all" approach to getting people into community.

Because I am an introvert by nature, I understand the fear that sets in with the thought of showing up at a stranger's house every week to share my deepest thoughts with a roomful of extroverts. I don't even want to share most of those thoughts with the people I am closest to! If we are going to convince people like me that small groups are beneficial, it's going to take a different approach. We have to be intentional about creating environments with the least amount of resistance.

Instead of forcing introverts to show up at our extroverted connect events, give them a few low-pressure options to joining groups. A sincere, extroverted staff member once suggested we put all the introverts to one side of the room and assign an extrovert to be their guide for the event, kind of like boys and girls at a middle-school dance. We didn't do that.

But here are a couple of connection strategies for introverts that have worked well:

- Give them an opportunity to fill out an information card on Sunday morning and drop it in the offering at the end of the service. Resist the temptation to force them to take it to a table in the lobby so they can "meet a groups staff member or a leader." First, that is an extra step that isn't necessary. Second, they may not yet be comfortable enough to talk to someone about groups. It was hard enough for them to take the first step of turning in the card.
- Provide a list of available and open groups on a website or in a book they can take home to look over. This gives them time to think through the options before committing to a group. I have found if given the proper space to make a decision about a group, most introverts will be all in. We are a loyal group of people.

Once they are connected to a group, if we are going to keep introverts beyond the first awkward meeting, our group leaders need to be trained differently. A majority of our training assumes everyone attending groups is ready to talk and begin community immediately. This is definitely not true for most introverts. Just like we need space to make a decision on joining a group, we need space to enter into the conversation once we are there.

One of our campus pastors at Seacoast Church visited a small group that was trying to think outside the box for their discussion. Their study for the semester was finding God in the movie *The Matrix*. After the normal small talk around snacks in the kitchen, the group gathered in the living room, where the leader took the first twenty minutes to actually act out one of the scenes from the movie, which included him playing every character and recreating all of the sound effects. The campus pastor reported back that the two other people in the group seemed frightened by the whole spectacle. That may not have been the *best* approach, but at least he was trying.

Food is always a good idea in a group, but especially for easing nervous people into the group. There is something mentally comforting about having a cup in your hand between you and the person on the other side of the conversation. Without the cup of joe, you kind of feel like Ricky Bobby in *Talladega Nights*: "I'm not sure what to do with my hands." It is amazing how a cheese-and-fruit tray will lower the anxiety level a few notches.

It's natural for a facilitator to attempt to get everyone in the group to talk right away. Most small-group studies are designed with an icebreaker question at the front to warm people up to the sound of their own voices. But introverts may not be ready to open up at the first meeting. They need to feel comfortable with the surroundings and the people before they're ready to jump into a conversation. The process could be quick, but it could also take a few meetings to reach that point. Forcing an introvert to talk is a sure way to not have them return the next week. Give them some room and they will eventually enter the discussions with precise and honest thoughts.

The best way for a small group to grab an introvert's attention is to move beyond the surface discussion and allow moments for well-thought-out dialogue. In her book *Quiet,* Susan Cain says of introverts: "They listen more than they talk, think before they speak, and often feel as if they express themselves better in writing than in conversation. They tend to dislike conflict. Many have a horror of small talk, but enjoy deep discussions."[1] Deeper discussions can come through giving the group a question to ponder during the week and come back to at the next meeting.

Introverts can be great small-group coaches. Coaching gives them a chance to spend some time with one person, doing more listening than talking, which is a skill that doesn't always come naturally to a lot of extroverts. When an introvert says she will pray and put some thought into it, you know she will do just that.

Introverts long for community in our churches, but we can't assume that existing routes will lead them there. Work on creating on-ramps designed for them, and they will be the most loyal members in your system.

Reaching Men

> Women speak because they wish to speak,
> whereas a man speaks only when driven to
> speech by something outside himself—like,
> for instance, he can't find any clean socks.
> —Jean Kerr, *The Snake Has All the Lines*

We have absolutely no problems with starting women's groups at Cross Point. Our connect events are full of tables with pink balloons signifying new women's groups. Men's groups, however, are a different story. A lot of guys' first impression of groups is they will be forced to be vulnerable and quite possibly hold hands with another person at some point during the meeting. Neither of those options appeal to most dudes.

If we are going to reach men with groups, we have to flip the stereotype. After all, the first biblical small group was a group of twelve guys who dropped everything to follow Jesus and change the world together. We need guys to believe it's possible to do that again.

When my family moved to Charleston to join the staff at Seacoast Church, our friends Sam and Joan invited us to attend their small group. I had never been part of a home group before and honestly had no interest in starting. I had all the typical fears about my manhood being stripped in a quick two-hour span on a Tuesday night. My nightmare would definitely end with a group hug after the closing prayer.

To my surprise, the first meeting wasn't that bad. No one invaded my introverted space, and not a single person asked me to share how I had sinned that week. In the conversation after the meeting, with a beverage cup tightly in my hand, Sam did something brilliant: he discovered that I was a musician and invited me to bring my guitar next week. Up to that moment I was trying to think through every excuse to not come back, but the thought of breaking out my axe trumped anything I could come up with. I returned the next Tuesday night with my acoustic in hand and have been immersed in group life for the eighteen years since then.

Sam tapped into something I was passionate about and used it to hook me into community. We had a common interest.

Finding those common interests is the key to reaching men. We need to stop expecting guys to give up who they are so they will conform to our vision of who they should be. Take a look at what a few dudes did in the Bible:

- David fought battles with his mighty men.
- Jesus took a group of fishermen and went fishing with them.
- Paul made tents with Aquila in Corinth.

Ask yourself, what are some common interests that guys already have to build biblical community around?

We have a men's group at Cross Point that gathers every Monday night during football season to watch the game and do their study during halftime. This group is so popular, it has multiplied several times. Their leader tapped into something that would happen organically and added God to it.

Another men's group has a common interest in cigars, so a group gets together weekly to smoke cigars and discuss the latest message from Sunday. I am not sure this is the healthiest approach to community, but it works. That group has also multiplied and is now fogging up several back porches around the Nashville area.

Give a group of men the freedom to add God to what they are already doing and there's no stopping them. How powerful could men's groups be if they discovered their purpose? They might just change the world—again.

Reaching Those People

Jesus heard this and said to them, "It is
not the healthy people who need a doctor,
but the sick. I did not come to invite
good people but to invite sinners."
—Mark 2:17

At Cross Point, everyone's welcome, nobody's perfect, and anything's possible. In fact, that's become our mantra. Once you've made the decision that everyone actually *is* welcome, it opens up an interesting question for small groups. Are groups a place where everyone is welcome too? If not, where do we draw the line?

We have a strong conviction that no one sin should disqualify a person from experiencing community. This is true particularly if you plan on placing groups as a front door to your church. To reach the fringes, it's going to get a little messy at times. Here are a few scenarios you may encounter if you haven't already done so:

- A person turns in a card on Sunday indicating they are new to the church and would like to join a small group as soon as possible. On the "Spouse" line of the card, they list a same-sex partner.
- A heterosexual couple signs up online for a couple's small group. You notice the home address is the same, but they are not listed as married and have different last names.
- A couple identifies themselves as gay and approaches the

small groups table after the service where the senior pastor has just asked for volunteers to host small groups over the next six weeks. They would like to host a group and invite their friends who don't attend church.

Is this where we draw the line on community? Do we ask them to get cleaned up first before they are allowed into our circles? You could, and a lot of churches do, but that's not the example Jesus gave us. He accepted all types of sinners into his inner circle before a lot of people would have allowed them in their church lobby.

Jesus took Simon, a guy with a major temper issue and known hater of Romans and tax collectors, and paired him up with Matthew, a tax collector.

He plucked a crooked tax collector out of a tree to host their traveling small group at his house that night.

He sat down late one night with Nicodemus, a Pharisee and a member of the Sanhedrin, to talk through what it means to be born again. Nicodemus later risked his life and reputation by standing up for Jesus in front of his fellow Pharisees and by helping Joseph of Arimathea take Jesus's body down from the cross and into the tomb.

Try to imagine the disciples' horror when Jesus made the decision to bring the woman at the well into the circle. Not only, according to Jewish custom, should Jesus have not spoken to a woman—much less a *Samaritan* woman—he started the conversation with bullet-pointing her multiple sins. Not exactly the icebreaker you would train your small-group leaders to lead with, but it worked pretty well for Jesus. The woman was not only accepted into the group but began inviting everyone she knew to check out the guy who knew everything about her.

Jesus created this crazy community out of people no one wanted anything to do with. As Pastor Pete says, "A lot of Christians would rather have conformity than community." We are uncomfortable with people with different sins from our sins. In order to reach the far fringes, we have to design our small-group systems with easy and obvious entry points for people who do not look, act, believe, or vote like us. This radical change in behavior starts with preparing our leaders to think differently.

Not every leader will be spiritually mature enough to navigate the conversations that will come from inviting gays into the group. Nor will every group be able to handle the possible disruption it could cause. A small-group point person has to be discerning to know which leaders are ready for the inevitable questions that will come from opening the group to everyone. If a leader is prepared and has those discussions with the group before it happens, the results can be amazing. If the leader is not spiritually mature and the group is not ready, it can ultimately destroy the group.

The popular church cliché is to "love the sinner but hate the sin." While it sounds nice, I don't believe it is biblical. Jesus gave us instructions with the ultimate commandment:

> "Teacher, which command in the law is the most important?"
>
> Jesus answered, "'Love the Lord your God with all your heart, all your soul, and all your mind.' This is the first and most important command. And the second command is like the first: 'Love your neighbor as you love yourself.' All the law and the writings of the prophets depend on these two commands." (Matthew 22:36–40)

We are asked to do two things: love God and love people. That's it. Jesus did not say, "Love your neighbor, but make sure to hate their sin." He just said to love them. What Jesus made simple we manage to make complicated. Billy Graham said, "It is the Holy Spirit's job to convict; it's God's job to judge; and it's our job to love."[2]

If you train your group leaders to provide an environment where people are loved and the gospel is shared, God and the Holy Spirit will take care of everything else. When those two things are done, biblical community will happen and lives will change.

A few years ago we approached two of our strongest leaders with a dilemma. A gay couple had requested a community group, and we thought that their midsize young professionals group might be a great fit. Would they consider praying and talking to their group about the possibility of allowing them to attend? They were unsure but agreed to take it to their group for a discussion. A week later they responded that the group had talked it over and decided there was no way they could *not* invite this couple into their group. A few weeks later the leaders told us that just having the conversation bonded the group like nothing had before. It brought them back to the original purpose of why we do what we do. Everyone is welcome, nobody's perfect, and anything is possible.

We recognized early on that just having our standard small-group options would not reach beyond the core of our church. We could continue placing people in groups who were brave enough to request them, but we would miss a large group of people not willing to wade through the process. That's when we decided to launch host groups, an idea we borrowed from Saddleback Church. With host groups, if you have a few friends, neighbors, or coworkers to invite to your home or conference room, you could facilitate a small group.

Offering another category of small groups gave more people the opportunity to add God to what they were already doing: gathering with friends in their everyday environments. In the two years we have offered the host group option, we have had non-Christians, gay couples, business leaders, apartment managers, touring bands, missionaries to China, and many, many more use our curriculum to start conversations about God with the people in their circles.

Opening the door to the fringes will not be clean and easy. We have to occasionally navigate issues that don't always bubble up to the surface in the typical small-group system. We have learned that walking alongside people whose lives are messy is hard. And it takes time. But if you put in the effort and stick with it, the stories of life change will follow. Here is an e-mail we received recently:

I just wanted to let you and your fellow staff members at Cross Point know how you have impacted our family. I will try to be brief.

My step-brother, who I love very much, is gay. We grew up in a small town in the South, so needless to say, that wasn't exactly the most accepting environment. In fact, he almost took his life in high school because the bullying was so brutal. He turned to drugs to mask the pain. When he was in his early 20s he moved to a large city looking for more acceptance. He found it. He also found bigger, badder drugs and many men. We thought we were going to lose him to a drug overdose and almost did several times.

Jeff eventually came home when he was 25 and we got him to attend a recovery group at church, where he found Christ. That's the good news. The bad news happened in his recovery small group. Somehow the topic of homosexuality came up, and the leader quickly said homosexuals are all going to hell. He had not told the group he was gay, so I guess they were surprised when he stood up, walked out, and never returned. In fact, he did not return to church until attending Cross Point last fall. He told me all about it. He said, "I just knew that God was the missing part of my life. So I asked a couple of friends what church I should go to and they both said Cross Point. So I tried it." He said, "You wouldn't believe it. It's like a rock concert with a band and smoke. The music is incredible. But the best part is that the pastor is like a real guy. He stands up there in his skinny jeans and talks. And I swear it's as if he has been with me all week long. It's like he is speaking straight to me." I asked him over Christmas, with fear and trembling, if he was still going. He said, "Oh, yes, I love it."

Can I just say, as the brother of a gay man, THANKS to you and the rest of the staff for making it a safe, loving environment for him. This shouldn't be rare for churches, but it is. Homosexuality is one of the messiest issues of our time, but bravo to you guys for showing love in mess!

—Thankful from a family you probably
didn't know you were reaching

Reaching the Least of These

Good works is giving to the poor and the
helpless, but divine works is showing them
their worth to the One who matters.
—Criss Jami

The site of our previous campus is on a fascinating line in West Nashville, just outside of downtown. We rented space from a Baptist church that at one time was one of the largest churches in the city. As the church grew, they had continued to add buildings until eventually the complex spanned an entire city block. The buildings seemingly had no relation to one another, and people could easily get lost trying to find their way through the maze of hallways and stairs. We suspect a few staff members got lost and never made it to the new campus when we moved a year ago. Cross Point utilized around 70 percent of the space, and the original congregation met in the rest.

The Baptist church began to decline when the surrounding once-quaint neighborhood changed, and the church did not change with it. The area declined economically, and 1980s suburban flight changed the landscape dramatically. The streets on one side of the church were quickly taken over by drug dealers and experienced nonstop violence. It's not a community where most people will willingly venture into after dark.

On the flip side, the regions immediately behind the church building have been revitalized over the last few years and are now one of the most desirable areas in town to live, eat, and shop. The building in which our church met was on the dividing line between an impoverished population and a wealthy gentry. If you attended one of our Sunday morning services, you might find yourself sitting between a country music star and a homeless person. It was a bizarre and beautiful mélange of cultures every weekend.

As we looked at our options for providing a holistic community as a church, we faced a difficult decision. We could continue on the easy route of staying on the safe side of the street, or we could step into the unknown on the other side. The Lord left us with an easy decision:

"I was hungry, and you gave me food. I was thirsty, and you gave me something to drink. I was alone and away from home, and you invited me into your house. I was without clothes, and you gave me something to wear. I was sick, and you cared for me. I was in prison, and you visited me."

Then the good people will answer, "Lord, when did we see you hungry and give you food, or thirsty and give you something to drink? When did we see you alone and away from home and invite you into our house? When did we see you without clothes and give you something to wear? When did we see you sick or in prison and care for you?"

Then the King will answer, "I tell you the truth, anything you did for even the least of my people here, you also did for me." (Matthew 25:35–40)

We have a mandate as Christ followers to take care of everyone in our path. The key to meeting needs is through relationships, but just opening our church buildings a few times a week is not enough. If we really believe that community is an option for everyone, then it is time for the church to get creative—and very uncomfortable.

In the six years we met at our first location, we began to forge relationships with organizations attempting to make a difference in the communities around us. These organizations included Preston Taylor Ministries, which provides a safe place for kids and families to learn in a Christian environment; Mending Hearts, a shelter for women who suffer with addiction and mental issues; and Lighthouse Ministries, a Christian-based substance abuse center for men. The relationship with Lighthouse Ministries led to the full-time use of one of their buildings on the edge of their property as a 24/7 Cross Point Dream Center.

The Dream Center exists not only as one of our campuses with Sunday morning programming but primarily as a Monday-through-Saturday light of hope to the poor and the powerless. The motto at the Dream Center is "Find a need and fill it." As we dreamed about what the Dream Center could be, we knew we would have to approach small groups in a different way. The system of recruiting host homes for launching new groups would not work in this community. A majority of the attenders walk to church on Sundays, or they are picked up and brought in by buses and vans. It was clear that the best option would be on-campus groups. But what types of groups would work best, and when would we host them?

Single Moms

As we looked at the needs of the community and the demographic of attenders on Sundays, it was clear that something for single moms was a huge need. The neighborhood is filled with struggling one-parent families who have given up hope of ever being more than what they currently are. Their only chance of crawling out of hopelessness was learning that they are not alone and that we will walk alongside them every step of the way. The best chance of changing the trajectory of this community is by reaching the kids, and that begins with their mothers.

We decided to launch a single-moms group that would meet for lunch after the final Sunday service in the back of the auditorium. An amazing volunteer took on the responsibility of leadership and began to build a team to feed and love on these women every week. People in the church caught the vision and began donating money to provide food and child care.

One of the single moms in the neighborhood heard about the group through our monthly community outreach and showed up one Sunday for the lunch. The group discovered that she had been a single mom for a long time and had lived a very difficult life with drugs and violence. After a few months of consistently attending the group, she started to pull her life together for the first time. Recently, the group leader decided to step back for a while, and this single mom is now leading this ministry. Her life would not have been the same if the leadership at the Dream Center had not taken a chance with launching this small-group community of single moms.

Exercise Groups

Our vision at the Dream Center is to reach the whole person, not only spiritually, but physically as well. We believe if we can help a person live a healthy lifestyle, they will have a better outlook on life. Each Wednesday at noon, the chairs are cleared out of the auditorium and an exercise video is shown on the big screen. Our Dream Center pastor has threatened to wear his yoga pants to the workout sessions, but we have convinced him so far that the sight would do more damage than any help exercise might otherwise overcome.

At one of our recent community events, our Dream Center coordinator invited one of the women in the neighborhood to attend the Wednesday workout group. She not only showed up but also brought two friends. She said, "All we do is sit around complaining about being out of shape and now we can work out next door for free!" They now all come to the exercise group almost every week, attend church on Sunday, and are involved in the single-moms group. The exercise group has now expanded to yoga sessions on Thursday afternoons, but we're still encouraging the Dream Center pastor to leave his tight pants at home.

Wednesday Night Q&A

After the Dream Center had been open for a few months, we noticed that a number of men who were part of the Lighthouse program were unable to attend Sunday morning services. Their program work schedule ties them up on Sundays, but they still wanted to be a part of the Cross Point community. We decided to launch a Wednesday night group during which we would not only play the video message from Sunday for the guys but also host a question and answer time to discuss the message.

The Wednesday night Q&A group quickly became popular and now consistently has forty to fifty guys attending. A worship leader in our church offered to lead a few songs to make the time a better worship experience for the guys. This midsize group is an ever-shifting community, bonding through discussion as to how the Sunday message applies to their lives. It will never look like our other message study groups, but that's okay.

We cannot turn a blind eye to the hurting all around us. Thomas Jefferson said, "If you want something you've never had, you must be willing to do something you've never done." It might be time to try something you've never done in order to reach those you've never reached.

Think It Over

- Who are we missing with our current connection strategies?
- What can we change to make it easier for introverts to be in community?
- What are some common interests we could use to rally men into groups?
- Is there a lifestyle or sin issue that should keep someone from being in a group?
- What kinds of issues might arise if we open community up to everyone?
- How can we design groups to reach those beyond the doors of our church?

3

Discipleship Is the Goal

The best measure of a spiritual life is
not its ecstasies but its obedience.
—Oswald Chambers

I am not a strong golfer. I love to watch golf, at least I have it on television while I nap, but there is little resemblance to what I have seen the pros do and what transpires when I am on a golf course. It's probably due to the overwhelming difference in talent and ability, but a lot of it comes down to strategy—or the lack of it. When Rory McIlroy steps up to the tee, he has a well-rehearsed strategy of what he is going to do next. He has visualized where the ball is going to go. His preshot routine is exactly the same every time he approaches the ball. He has practiced his swing so many times that each shot looks almost identical in form. He has spent hours and hours planning his strategy and practicing before he even steps onto a golf course.

My approach to golf is simple: I swing hard, close my eyes, and hope for the best. This strategy works about three or four times a round, at best. The rest of the time it's just awful. I could probably be a decent golfer if I would work on a strategy to hitting the ball, but I have not put in the reps on the practice range to make it happen.

This is the same strategy a lot of churches and pastors follow for a discipleship plan. We don't really understand what it should look like, so we swing hard, close our eyes, and hope for the best.

You may be a pastor who believes a disciple of Christ should possess a lot of biblical knowledge. In their book *Transformational Groups*, Ed Stetzer and Eric Geiger found that 56 percent of pastors with a discipleship plan list biblical knowledge as their first priority.[1] So you add more discipleship classes to pass down volumes of information. Once attendees have made it through all the classes, they should have enough knowledge to be called a disciple. This approach, however, often results with people who are educated far beyond their level of obedience.

Or you may decide a disciple should always be on mission, because knowledge will come through doing the work. The training is based on active ministry outside the walls of the church, not in its classrooms. This strategy can lead to a group of eternal baby Christians without the foundation needed to defend their beliefs.

After looking at these options, you may conclude that starting a bunch of small groups is the answer to discipleship. But groups are just a tool for creating disciples, and they will never be an effective one without an intentional plan to measure spiritual growth. According to Stetzer and Geiger, "Only 43 percent of the pastors surveyed said their church regularly evaluates discipleship progress among their congregation."[2] The rest are swinging hard, closing their eyes, and hoping for the best.

If we look at Jesus's example for creating disciples, we see that it was simple but intentional. "Come, follow me," he said, "and I will make you fish for people" (Matthew 4:19). Jesus was calling very common men to spend time with him on mission. The disciples were gaining knowledge by spending time with Jesus and one another. There was intentionality and movement in Jesus's strategy.

Before you implement a strategy to make disciples, you have to first define what a disciple is. Just like a professional golfer, you have to envision what the end result of a shot will be. Finish this statement for your church: A follower of Christ is _____. What will a fully devoted follower of Christ at your church be like?

As I have wrestled with this question for our groups, I have landed on this working definition: *Followers of Christ are striving to become more like Jesus in every aspect of their life.* If a disciple is becoming more like Jesus, it takes intentional movement. No one gets there by accident.

Movement Toward God

Jesus's first words to Simon and his brother Andrew were, "Come follow me." As you think about the disciples' journey with Jesus, you can picture them following him, always striving to take their next steps to come closer to the Master. But all of them moving at their own pace and rhythm. One mistake we make as leaders is the assumption that everyone is on the same pace in their journey with Christ. Thus we need to design pathways for these steps without regulating what those steps are.

My wife and I realized pretty early that our first child, Brianna, was going to be special. Like all first-time parents, we had high hopes for our firstborn. My first birthday gift for her was a basketball and a goal. A future professional basketball player has to start somewhere, right? But it became clear that sports might not be her only future path when she started talking when she was one year old. I don't mean a few cute words here and there, but complete thoughts about everything. We had to ask her to not talk at the airport, because there was no way the authorities would believe she was under two years old and qualified to be a lap child. Brianna started reading on her own at three, with complete books under her belt by four. Her progress has continued at this pace all the way through high school. She is always at the top of her class in almost every subject. Although she works very hard at it, learning seems almost effortless for her.

By the time our second child came along five years later, we thought we had this parenting thing down. Ashlyn was not only going to follow in her big sister's footsteps, but we now had the knowledge to help her surpass Brianna's accomplishments. But it didn't exactly work out that way. Ashlyn is very intelligent and makes great grades in school, but she has to work extremely hard at it. Her personality is also the opposite of her sister's. The guidance we gave Brianna to succeed has to be different for Ashlyn. She would rather socialize first and then learn. Brianna starts everything in her life with a book.

We make the same assumptions about people's spiritual growth. We create classes and requirements to keep people on the same path toward Jesus. This strategy makes for straight lines on paper, but spiritual formation doesn't always lay out in pretty, straight lines. No two people move toward Jesus in the exact same way.

I was born with an abnormally large noggin. I would love to believe it's because of my abnormally large brain, but my test scores proved that not to be the case. Other than stretching out my share of turtleneck shirts in the 1990s, having a large head is not really an issue until I start shopping for hats. I have learned to stay away from the "one size fits all" section because that claim is a big, fat lie. The makers of those hats have obviously never put a measuring tape around my ginormous head.

Discipleship, too, is not a "one size fits all" process. Instead of forcing people to fit into our spiritual boxes, we should be helping people to discover what the next step is for them and what they need to do to take it. Small-group leaders need to be taught to constantly look for spiritual signals from their members. Sometimes those signals are obvious, but most of the time they are more difficult to spot.

I typically ask for prayer requests at the end of the discussion time during our small-group meetings. I try to switch up how we pray and will occasionally ask for different people to take one of the requests and lift it up in prayer in front of the group.

I noticed that one of the guys in our group had never offered to pray for a request. I was okay with that, because praying in front of a group is not always easy for everyone. One night near the end of the semester, he pulled me to the side as we headed in for the discussion and said, "I got this tonight."

Not quite understanding what he meant, I said, "Okay, but what are you talking about?"

He said, "I have never prayed in front of anyone in my life, but I think I can do it tonight. I will take one of the requests when we have prayer time."

I said, "That's great, but you really don't have to. There's nothing wrong with praying to yourself for the requests. God will hear it either way."

He looked at me a little dismayed and said, "No. I need to do this. This is a huge step for me, and I need to take it."

That night, he took one of the requests, and when he saw me after group, he beamed and said, "Told you I got it!"

Praying out loud at a small-group meeting may not be most people's next spiritual step, but it was Brian's that night. To measure if the groups at your church are moving toward God, ask these questions:

- Are we training our leaders to listen for spiritual signals from their group members?
- Are new groups being started with leaders being raised up within existing groups?
- Are there stories of life changes coming out of the groups?

Movement Toward One Another

The transliterated Greek word for the term "each other" is *allelon*, and it's used fifty-eight times in the New Testament. Here are just a few uses of the term:

- "Meet together and encourage each other" (Hebrews 10:25)
- "Encourage each other" (1 Thessalonians 4:18)

- "Love each other like brothers and sisters" (Romans 12:10)
- "By helping each other with your troubles, you truly obey the law of Christ" (Galatians 6:2)
- "Care the same for each other" (1 Corinthians 12:25)
- "Pray for each other" (James 5:16)
- "Serve each other with love" (Galatians 5:13)
- "Forgive each other" (Colossians 3:13)

It becomes clear as you read through the Bible that we were not meant to walk through this life on our own. I am convinced that it's possible to achieve community without discipleship, but it's impossible to achieve discipleship without community. The original small group spent a majority of their time taking care of one another's needs. As Andy Stanley says, they were constantly "one anothering one another."[3]

An effective small-group leader creates an environment where basic needs are met within the group. The first call should never be to the church office or a local agency; it should always be to the small group.

This is exactly what happened to one of our young-adult group leaders and now staff member, Wes Howard. Here is his story:

A few years ago, I rented a cabin to get away with God to try and get some clarity on a nudging I had been feeling about my job and career path. The next day I went to work after the cabin trip, I lost my job. The day after that, I attended my first community group at Cross Point. Talk about crazy timing.

Six months later, the severance package had just about run out. I was job-searching big time but unfortunately had come in second place on several opportunities. My community group was well aware of everything and was a great source of encouragement to me. Spiritually, I was growing more than I ever had before in my entire life. There came a point where I would not have enough money to pay my rent. I did not tell anyone this. I was just praying and frantically job searching.

The week the rent was due, I went to group like normal, and at the end of the night, the leader stood up and told me how much they loved me and believed in me and that they wanted to make sure that I knew that. She handed me an envelope and inside was a check. It was the exact amount of my rent, and my rent was a weird number. You couldn't have easily guessed it. In that moment, I knew that I was right where God wanted me to be.

Wes's trajectory was changed because his small group followed God's prompting to take care of one of their own. Discipleship does not happen by accident or in a vacuum. It takes a community of believers who are always looking out for one another. As leaders, we need to be intentional about looking for the one-another stories and celebrating them with other group leaders.

To measure if your groups are taking care of one another, think about these questions:

- Are they taking meals to other group members when a baby is born or someone has a death in the family?
- Are they the first responders when there is an emergency, and a group member ends up in the hospital?
- Are they pooling their resources when a group member suddenly loses a job and needs assistance for a short period?

Movement Toward Mission

The final act for Jesus with his disciples was to send them out to do the work on their own. They had spent time following in his footsteps and building community, but it was time to take what they had learned and begin to spread it across the world.

> [Jesus] called his twelve disciples to him and gave them authority to drive out impure spirits and to heal every disease and sickness. . . .
>
> These twelve Jesus sent out with the following instructions: "Do not go among the Gentiles or enter any town of the Samaritans. Go rather to the lost sheep of Israel. As you go, proclaim this message: 'The kingdom of heaven has come near.' Heal the sick, raise the dead, cleanse those who have leprosy, drive out demons. Freely you have received; freely give." (Matthew 10:1, 5–8, NIV)

Jesus is telling his group, "I have given you all of this divine knowledge. Now it's time to give it away." Our small groups need easy and obvious paths to take what they are learning and give it away. As you design your systems, look for low-level entry points to allow groups to live out what they are learning. Here are a few opportunities we have at Cross Point for groups to serve together in missions:

- *Neighborhood parties:* We encourage our leaders and hosts to invite people in their circles of influence to group before inviting them to a Sunday service. Their unchurched friends and neighbors are more likely to take that first step if it's an invitation to a home and not a church building. We give our leaders some tools to help make the invitation process a little easier. Each host packet includes custom invitations to distribute to their neighbors and video training on how to make the big ask. We also encourage our groups to host neighborhood block parties during the summer. We provide a block party kit with banners, yard signs, invitations, door hangers, ideas for games and food, kids' activities, a music playlist link, party favors, and a notebook for writing down the names and contact information for a follow-up invitation to dinner.

• *Serving Saturdays:* Several times a year we help organize community projects throughout our city for our church to venture out and serve en masse. If you drive around Nashville on one of our Serving Saturdays, you'll see red "Serve" T-shirts everywhere. Our groups serve at local schools, AIDS clinics, food pantries, women's shelters, homeless shelters, community cleanups, other churches, and anywhere where we can make a difference. There are no strings attached to our serving. We only want to show who Christ is through acts of kindness around our community. Serving Saturday is a great vehicle for groups to serve together.

• *Short-term missions trips:* There is nothing that changes a person's worldview more than spending a week on a mission trip in a developing country. We sponsor trips throughout the year to the Dominican Republic, Haiti,

Honduras, India, and Kenya. A small group that spends a week together in service in another country is guaranteed to come back ready to do anything to make a difference in the world.

Every August, our pastor does a DNA vision series where he lays out who we are as a church and why we do what we do. The first week is about discipleship, the second week is on community, and the third week is why we do missions. A couple of years ago, we decided that instead of just telling the church why we do global missions, we would show them. We quickly arranged a "Where in the world is Pete?" trip where the pastor and a camera crew hit all five of our international partners (the Dominican Republic, Haiti, Honduras, India, and Kenya) in eight days. On the Sunday of the mission's emphasis week, we used the video to give people a visual of where we serve around the world.

The service was very effective, and immediately record numbers of people signed up to go for the first time for one of our fifteen short-term missions trips the next year. Five members of a young-adult group were there that day, and they each individually felt the tug to go on a trip but were too intimidated by the idea of signing up. When they met as a group later that night, they began to talk about the idea of going on a trip and the fears they had about signing up. By the end of the meeting, they collectively decided to go to Haiti on the next available trip. They did everything as a group to get ready for it, from having yard sales to helping with fund-raising, to holding packing parties together before the trip. The fear that was there individually was erased in the context of a group. That trip to Haiti changed the direction of those small-group members' lives because they chose to be on mission together.

We encourage new groups to form after members return from a mission trip. They have seen what the power of community can do when focused on doing good for eight days. Imagine what could happen if small groups poured that same energy into their own communities.

- *Adopt-a-Blocks:* An idea passed on to us from the Dream Center in Los Angeles is that of loving your community one block at a time.[4] Every first Saturday of the month, people from Cross Point gather in small groups to go door-to-door, finding needs and filling them. One month might be basic trash cleanup. The next month might be offering household items like light bulbs. At Thanksgiving time, they might take meals to homes that would otherwise go without for the holiday. This all culminates in a block party in the parking lot of the Cross Point Dream Center at noon.

What makes Adopt-a-Blocks work is consistency and community. Everything and everyone else come and go on those streets, so we are determined to stay. The same small groups hit the same blocks every month. After two years of persistent helping, doors that would never open in the beginning are now not only opening to our groups, but the people behind them are participating in the event as well.

Very slowly, life change is taking place because those small groups will not go away.

Give groups a list of local organizations to partner with. Lower the intimidation bar on taking an international missions trip. Organize periodic church-wide serving opportunities around the city. Make groups aware of the different serving opportunities within the church. To measure whether your groups are living missionally, ask these questions:

- Are they going on short-term missions trips together?
- Are they periodically serving together somewhere in their community?
- Are they inviting their neighbors into their group?
- Are they serving somewhere in the church together?

It Takes Time

One reason it's difficult to measure discipleship in your church is because it is a hard and lengthy process. Seeing life change take place takes a lot of time and deliberate effort from leaders willing to invest in life-on-life relationships. We have grown accustomed to expecting immediate results. If a new initiative is not producing instant fruit, we cut it. If a new idea is not embraced by the majority, we drop it. If a person in our group takes a step back in their walk, we move on.

But sustained life change can sometimes take months or years before it's fully realized in someone's life. I always cringe when I hear about celebrities who have recently turned their life over to God and are now being paraded as an example on television. They still need a *lot* of time and refining before finding their spiritual footing.

One of our group leaders at Cross Point told me recently that he has been investing in a group member for years with very little fruit so far to show for it. In fact, if he's not careful during a group discussion, this person can start to swing the conversation the wrong direction and sway the group of primarily new Christians off track. But he said, "I will continue to pour into this person for as long as it takes." This leader understands the power of persistence.

Paul recognized the power of persistence when he addressed the Christians in Corinth:

> Brothers and sisters, in the past I could not talk to you as I talk to spiritual people. I had to talk to you as I would to people without the Spirit—babies in Christ. The teaching I gave you was like milk, not solid food, because you were not able to take solid food. And even now you are not ready. (1 Corinthians 3:1–2)

How many times have we expected our baby Christians to be on solid food when they're only capable of digesting 2 percent milk? Solid food looks great on the stats sheet. We believe disciples on solids are easier to take care of. Less crying. Fewer missteps. But change does not happen overnight.

As I sat down with a friend for coffee, he began to share with me the reason why he had lost faith in the church. After weekly Bible studies for two years at his previous church, his spiritual partner sat him down one day and explained how he would have to leave the church immediately because they were not seeing enough fruit in his life. The change they felt needed to take place in his spiritual walk was taking too much time for the relationship to continue. It was time to move on.

When I asked him what had brought him to church at Cross Point, he said, "I have never felt the pressure to be anything else than what I am at Cross Point. I am allowed to grow at my own pace. It's truly okay to not be okay."

Spiritual maturity is not just another box on a checklist. If discipleship is really the goal for our small groups, it's going to take the long game to get it done. We cannot walk away from relationships when they start to become inconvenient for us.

Curriculum Matters

Curriculum will not always guarantee discipleship, but a solid, biblically based study plan can help group leaders lay the foundation for spiritual growth. Although we allow our groups at Cross Point to choose their own curriculum, most new leaders and hosts struggle with what their group should be studying next. We get very little pushback when we ask our groups to study the same thing twice a year in conjunction with our church-wide campaigns. They appreciate having the guidance and the church removing the guesswork for curriculum choices. We have to remember that group leaders have full-time jobs and don't necessarily have enough time to scour local Christian bookstores for bits and pieces of a Bible study.

To help ease the decision-making process and to provide a discipleship path for our groups, we created a curriculum menu. The menu includes categories titled "Appetizers," "Salads," "Main Courses," "A la Carte," and "Desserts." Each category has five to six curriculum choices that have been tested by experienced leaders and proven to be good options. If the leaders pick one study from each category for a year, their group will have a full discipleship diet of curriculum.

Unlike an actual restaurant, appetizers and salads are not necessarily lighter in content than the main courses, but they are easier to manage studies to start out with a new group. Most of them are DVD driven, so the leader doesn't have to worry about creating content each week. All of our church-wide studies fall under the appetizer category. We also include a couple of studies that are targeted toward new believers in this section. *Starting Point* by Andy Stanley and North Point Church[5] is a great ten-week study for new Christ followers and even nonbelievers.

Main courses cover the core fundamentals of who we are as a church with studies focusing on evangelism, discipleship, and community. Like the salads and appetizers, most of these are DVD based but give seasoned leaders the option of shouldering more of the content if they desire.

The dessert category has fun options for our groups to consider through the course of a semester. We encourage all of our groups to take occasional breaks from the studies and do something fun together as a group. A group that has fun together will grow together. These options include:

- Hosting a game night.
- Going to a baseball game.
- Meeting for a picnic in the park.
- Going kayaking.
- Taking the group camping over the weekend.

A la carte options are studies for specific demographic groups, like men, women, marriage, preparation for marriage, and so forth.

The majority of the studies on the menu are four to six weeks long. Most groups could make it through each category in a year and then repeat the rotation with different studies. We update the study choices yearly to keep it fresh with new options.

While curriculum does not guarantee discipleship, it does give a foundation for a leader to start the necessary conversations. We discovered that groups who stay with the same category of studies for more than two years begin to hear the same answers to the same questions. Having a curriculum menu introduces different perspectives on the same spiritual topics. It also gives the church leadership a handle on what is being taught through the groups.

Discipleship-Focused Groups

I was tasked a couple of years ago with developing a process for ordaining people as pastors at Cross Point. As I began to research the possibilities, I realized there was not a clear path for those who desired to be in ministry and wanted to grow in their understanding of the Bible. I was driven by Paul's comment to Timothy: "Do your best to present yourself to God as one approved, a worker who does not need to be ashamed and who correctly handles the word of truth" (2 Timothy 2:15, NIV). We had plenty of Bible studies available through our groups, but nothing to immerse an aspiring pastor in deeper theology. We were not preparing them to correctly handle the word of truth.

The option to attend a seminary isn't a practical choice for most church attendees or staff, so I put together a six-month crash course in systematic theology and modern church philosophy and practices. Each month a group member would study a bit of systematic theology along with a book about spiritual leadership in the church. I would occasionally have guest pastors sit in with the group to give their perspective on the topic for that month. There are also online assignments to go along with the topic (interview a local pastor, build a Bible study, write a message, etc.) to help put what they're reading into practice along the way. The format for the group is based on open dialogue, not lectures from a teacher.

We launched the program with a small pilot group of staff members and have now expanded it to handpicked emerging leaders from our different campuses. The plan is to eventually open it to the whole church, with several spiritual leadership groups running throughout the year.

Out of the success of the spiritual leadership group, we have now developed an organizational leadership group based on the same format. This group focuses more on the core principles for overall leadership; the systematic theology component is not used.

It's All About Balance

When a golfer reaches the tipping point of going from weekend hacker to having a legitimate game, it's because he's managed to perfect the nuances that go into a good golf swing without thinking about it. There is a balance to the stance, the take away, the approach, and the follow-through.

Creating disciples who make disciples is not about focusing only on one aspect of discipleship; it's striving for a balance of teaching, listening, refining, and doing. Examine your current discipleship strategy and note how balanced you are with your offerings. Are you focused just on teaching or are there opportunities for living it out? Are your groups digging below the surface or are they functioning more as social clubs? Finding that balance will change the way your church thinks about discipleship.

Think It Over

- What is your current discipleship strategy?
- If you do not have a discipleship strategy, what is the first step for implementing one?
- How are you measuring spiritual growth through your small groups?
- What opportunities are you offering people to live out what they're learning?

A Clean Slate

That last page turned is a perfect
excuse to write a whole new book.
—Toni Sorenson

With one exception, every home my wife and I have owned has been new construction. We love the opportunity to help create space that functions best around how we live. We also somehow manage to always move when it's almost time for major repairs to kick in: new water heater, new roof, new appliances, new flooring. We never had to face any of those until we moved to Nashville. Our first house in Music City was twelve years old and on the verge of needing new everything.

Because of my extreme lack of handyman skills, most of the needed repairs were dragged out until we couldn't take it anymore and decided to move into a newly constructed house in the downtown section of the city. Our buyer's inspection report pointed out several issues we had been dreading. The sixteen-year-old water heater was on its last legs. The roof needed to be replaced. Almost every window on the first floor was too ancient to properly insulate the house. It was clear that if we were going to sell this house, several functioning systems would have to be replaced or redone.

We face a similar dilemma with tried-and-true systems in our churches. As leaders, we love to hold on to our structures with everything we have. Any sign of change can look and feel like failure. What we don't see is, if we don't change them now, we won't actually realize failure until it's obvious to everyone.

Blow It Up

In a growing church, every system should be tweaked or completely blown up every few years. If it's a fast-growing church, that may be as quick as every one to two years. No matter how highly functioning a system is, it will have to evolve to keep up with changing cultures and growth. What worked to get people into groups at a church of two hundred attenders will not always be as effective with five hundred attenders.

Sometimes those changes may be small tweaks that can make a big difference. We have never had a problem getting people to sign up for groups at Cross Point. Our pastor does an amazing job of making an appeal twice a year and selling the benefit of being in community with other people. As soon as he is finished, people have the opportunity to indicate they would like to join a small group.

During my first push for groups at Cross Point, we saw over fourteen hundred people respond favorably. We worked hard to get those people into groups, but only a small percentage of those people responded when group leaders contacted them with details about a group. Even though we sent e-mails to the fourteen hundred within forty-eight hours of their signing up for groups, most of them never replied.

After a couple of sign-up campaigns with similar results, we decided to tweak our response system to see if people would respond differently. Instead of sending e-mails welcoming them to the group community, everyone on staff called everyone who indicated a desire to join a group who gave us their phone number. We were not able to reach every person, but we left voice mails thanking them for signing up and letting them know we were working to plug them into a great group. The response to this small change in approach was huge. The people we talked to were surprised we would take the time to call them. Not only did our rate of response go way up, but we were able to pray with people and heard incredible stories of life change during the process. Just making the decision to go old school with phone calls made a sizable difference in participation.

Sometimes, though, it's not a small tweak but a complete reconstruction that's needed. One of my first goals at Cross Point was to implement a coaching system for our leaders. I knew there was no way for our staff (I was the only full-time groups staff member at the time) to give adequate care for all of our leaders as we developed.

We decided the best ratio would be somewhere around one coach for every three to five leaders. Any more than that would be too much for a volunteer to shoulder throughout a semester.

We began recruiting as many good coaches as we could find. We started with the most successful small-group leaders who headed large groups. We understood that if they could build a large group, they could likely handle coaching some other leaders at the same time. One of my first recruits was Chris Nichols (who is now pastor of our Bellevue campus) and his wife, Stephanie, who is on our groups staff. He immediately turned me down. This should have been a warning sign.

It didn't take long to figure out that the coaching system wasn't working. Here are three discoveries we made along the way:

1. *Great small-group leaders do not always make great coaches.* The skill set needed to gather a large group of people every week is not the same as mentoring other leaders.
2. *Most of the people we chose were already maxed out with leading their group.* They did not have any time to invest in guiding other leaders, especially not a few hours every week on top of their present workload.
3. *Even though we believed our current leaders would welcome having another leader occasionally check on them, we discovered that was not the case.* A majority of the veteran leaders did not see the need to be coached.

We could either continue to make tweaks to try to force a coaching system to work or blow it all up and start over. We went with the latter. Even though everything looked great on paper, we decided to take a completely different approach to coaching.

- Instead of requiring every leader to have a coach at all times, we asked only new leaders to have a coach for at least the first semester. We gave our veteran leaders the option of having one. They could opt out at any time.
- Instead of going after our most successful group leaders, we looked for potential coaches who would work well in a one-on-one mentoring relationship. We realized our most successful coaches did not have to be group leaders themselves, thus they would have time to work with other leaders.
- We adjusted the time requirements for coaching to make it more accessible for volunteers. Our coaches are not tasked with being a small-group police. They don't take attendance or show up at groups to make sure they are functioning correctly. They exist as a support system for the leaders.

We termed this new approach *as-needed coaching*. Ever since we instituted these guidelines, we have seen a much higher acceptance from both our leaders and potential coaches. It would not be true to say this concept is exactly where we would like it to be, but we are definitely moving in the right direction.

Whether you are starting from scratch at a brand-new church plant or blowing up a large system at an existing church, there are some principles that can help set up your new plan for success down the road. Here are seven guidelines to think through.

1. Define the Win

When our oldest daughter was in kindergarten, she decided to try out for soccer. There may have been a little pressure from her dad to play a sport, but that is beside the point. I played a few sports in high school and am very competitive by nature. My daughter is not. At her soccer games, Brianna decided it was more fun to pick daises than chase a stupid ball. But what drove me crazy was the fact that no one kept score during the games. I could not figure out how you could celebrate at the end of the game when no one had won! I now understand that the win was just playing the game, but again, that's not the point.

Every ministry has to decide what its *win* looks like, and this is especially true for groups. If you don't know what success looks like, how can you celebrate it? As you dream about what groups could look like at your church, start with the end in mind. What results would you like to see if your system works perfectly? Andy Stanley says, "Your system is perfectly designed to get the results you're getting."[1] If my church is not producing disciples, there's probably a systems problem. If only a small percentage of the congregation is involved in groups, it's probably a systems issue. If we are not developing enough leaders to keep up with our growth, it probably has something to do with our leadership development system.

We spend a lot of time as leaders taking on the next problem that pops up rather than dreaming about what the future could look like. A clean slate gives you the white board space to create those end goals.

- What percentage of adult attenders would you like to see connected to groups? It's easy to think that we want the answer to be 100 percent, but what is a realistic yet audacious goal to put out in front of your leaders and congregation? If your current rate is 15 percent, taking it to 50 percent with the next campaign is a worthy goal. Keep that 100 percent goal as a three- to four-year goal, but celebrate each milestone step along the way.

- How many groups would you need to start to reach your next goal? We can say we want 80 percent of our adult attenders in groups, but it cannot happen without the groups in which to put additional people. If the ideal size for a small group at your church is ten to fifteen people, calculate how many groups you would need based on your expected growth. Group launches work best during natural growth seasons at a church: fall (back to school), January (New Year's resolutions), and Easter.

- How many leaders do you need to develop to lead those new groups? Now is the time to start thinking through what your leadership pipeline is going to look like for producing new leaders. Decide how high you are going to set the bar for leadership and what kind of training is needed to set them up for success.

- How many coaches would you need to guide those new leaders? A functioning coaching system is the hardest piece to get right, but the entire system will crumble without proper care for your untested leaders. Don't give up on coaching early. Give it time and space to develop.

- What does a developing disciple look like at your church? Remember that community is key, but discipleship is the goal. Spend time with your team considering how you can measure spiritual growth within small groups. If you do not measure it, you will never be able to celebrate it.

2. Choose a Champion

I talk to a lot of small-group pastors who cannot get any traction with groups at their churches. They want to know how we have been able to get our people at Cross Point to buy into the idea of community. The first question I ask is, Is your senior pastor in a small group? Almost every time the answer is "no."

It's not impossible to build a successful groups system without the senior leader being fully on board, but it's extremely difficult. The congregation is going to take its cues from the leaders, and if the senior pastor is not engaged in community, they will follow his lead. It does not matter how much he talks about the importance of groups from the pulpit if there are not consistent stories circulating from his own small group.

Our senior pastor constantly talks about what his small group means to him. He will casually throw a story into a Sunday message that references something from his group that past week. That one story carries more weight than if I gave an entire message on a Sunday about groups.

I have seen Pastor Rick Warren do this for years. The number-one reason why Saddleback Church consistently has more than 100 percent of their attendance in small groups is because Rick will not be quiet about groups. I have never seen a message from Saddleback that did not reference small groups at some point.

Notice, however, I did not say that the senior leader has to *lead* a small group for people to follow him. In fact, I believe most senior pastors are terrible small-group leaders. We teach our group leaders that it is okay to not have all the answers. They are there to facilitate a conversation, not teach a lesson. Pulling that off is almost impossible for a pastor who is accustomed to teaching every weekend. Lead pastors cannot stand the silence required after a question is asked for people to jump into the conversation. Most teaching pastors have an uncontrollable desire to fill dead air with something thought provoking. It's just in their nature.

It is also healthy for the pastor to be willing to give up control and just be in a group for a while. He should be allowed to handpick the group so that it is a place where he can feel safe sharing his life. Also, a pastor should not feel any pressure to always be on, especially in his own small group. His small group may include people who are not members of the church. As long as they are experiencing community and growing spiritually, the rest of the church will follow.

While it's not necessary for the senior pastor to lead his own group, it is vital that he takes the lead for small groups as a whole. A lot of pastors make the mistake of delegating the role of the small-group champion to a staff member. If groups are pushed on the stage at all, it always comes from the small-groups staff member. While a church does need an *expert* to help form strategy and structures, the role of groups champion should always be the senior leader of the congregation.

Another common mistake in a lot of churches where small groups are not working is that the job of overseeing groups is delegated either to a committee (several staff members sharing the load between them) or it is one responsibility among many for a single staff member. No one in the church is waking up every day thinking about how to get more people into biblical community.

If your goal is to become a church *of* small groups, it requires intentionality and absolute focus from the leadership. Small groups will always struggle if the responsibility is relegated to an already overworked student pastor. At the same time, the groups point person does not always have to fall on the shoulders of a full-time staff member. There are high-capacity volunteers in your church who are passionate about seeing people discipled. All they need is a vision from leadership and the resources to carry it out.

3. Put It in the Budget

When it comes down to budgeting for small groups, a lot of churches follow the example of Pharaoh in Exodus:

> That same day the king gave a command to the slave masters and foremen. He said, "Don't give the people straw to make bricks as you used to do. Let them gather their own straw. But they must still make the same number of bricks as they did before. Do not accept fewer." (Exodus 5:6–8)

We are asking our point people for groups to build a successful system without the necessary straw but still expecting big results. As much as we want to believe community happens organically, it still takes resources for them to be strategic and effective. Here are a few things to think about as you plan out a budget for groups:

- *Put money in for staff and coaches to take leaders out for lunch or coffee.* Meetings can happen anywhere, but there is something about sitting down for coffee that engenders honest conversation. Do not limit this to staff. Make sure your coaches have the means to meet with their leaders.

- *Do not skimp on the database or website.* Everything around us is moving online and going mobile, so that is where people will expect to look for groups. There is great software available that will tie your church database to your website. If your congregation cannot find information about a group from their phone, it may as well not exist.

- *Budget for at least one nice evening every year to appreciate your group leaders.* Your leaders spend a lot of time and effort throughout the year cleaning and opening their homes as meeting places every week. Take one night to show them how much you appreciate it. Make sure to serve them really good food.

- *Put enough money aside to make first-class signs and printed materials.* If you are planning to host any kind of small-groups fair/connection event, you will need some collateral to support it. Make it look the best you can. Brand it all in the same way. *Please* do not use handwritten material. People will know immediately how much you value your groups by the quality of your materials.

- *Even if you cannot currently pay someone to be a full-time staff member over groups, start putting it on the wish list for your budget.* Your groups will grow exponentially if there is someone on the organizational chart who thinks about them every day.

4. Make It Scalable

When we launched a campus in a nearby city, we could not find a suitable building for them to meet in. Property in this area is expensive, and it seemed like every rental possibility fell through. The campus ended up meeting at a school for the first two years, but it was extremely small. The auditorium was the library because the school did not have a theater or a gym. Our tech team did an amazing job of disguising it with drapes, but it was still the size of a small school library.

The lack of space limited the growth of the campus and the number of small groups. Then, out of nowhere, we received an e-mail from a church that was considering shutting down their campus in this same area. They polled us about our interest in taking over their building. The structure was in an ideal part of town, and the church's theology and methodology aligned with ours. After conversations and much praying, we moved our campus into their building. The other church officially closed, and Cross Point opened in its place. Within a week, campus attendance tripled! It was the result of our moving into a permanent building along with many people from the previous congregation staying on.

While we were elated about the sudden growth, the growth exposed holes in our systems. We were not prepared in groups to provide community for that many people. We were scrambling (and still

are) to find leaders to start new groups. Our volunteer groups directors were overwhelmed with the need to care for the number of people
who were suddenly requesting groups.

Your church may never triple in size overnight (although it could),
but now is the time to start planning for God to do the unexpected.
What happens when you activate your first all-church campaign and
suddenly need to triple the number of current groups to meet the
demand? Do you have enough coaches? How difficult is it to become
a small-group leader? Can you fast-track the vetting of new leaders?
You should always be ready to go when God moves.

5. Make It Replicable

As a multisite church (one church in several locations), we are constantly thinking about how ministries will work in buildings of
varying sizes and in different cultures. For instance, what works well
in an urban setting may not fly in a rural context. Our Nashville
campus sits in the heart of downtown. The majority of attenders
are young, single professionals. And we are struggling to keep up
with necessary numbers of young professional groups needed by that
campus.

We decided to experiment with an open group that would never
close but continue starting new small groups within the larger group.
They eventually needed their own system of coaches and leadership
training to keep up with the growth. This midsize group started with
four people at an offsite location but quickly grew to over two hundred young adults who met in the gym at the Nashville campus.

Our initial attempts to replicate the success of this midsize group did not work as well at other campuses. The setting and demographics of the Nashville campus were perfect for a young-adults group, but attempting to copy it around the city did not make sense. Instead of giving up on the midsize group concept, the other campuses' group directors experimented with different types of groups and formats. Cross Point now has successful midsize moms', men's, and women's groups. They don't all look exactly the same, but they are all based on our small-group expectations regarding evangelism, community, and service.

Think through not only what could be replicable across different locations, but also what small groups look like in different layers of your church. The heart of our students' and kids' ministries are small groups. My eleven-year-old has had the same small-group leaders since she was in first grade. She refuses to attend another service on Sundays because she would miss spending time with the two group leaders she has known for five years. Her guest list for birthdays are friends, family, and her small-group leaders.

The student service on Wednesday nights is considered a warm-up for the small-group time that follows. I know of at least one megachurch that has canceled its student programming and switched exclusively to weekly small groups.

Those ministries can benefit from partnering with the adult groups system for training, leadership development, and structure ideas. What if the same team that develops Sunday message studies works with the student leaders on theirs? What if a few adult group leaders mentor small-group leaders in the kids' ministry? Replicating successful systems will help break down silos within a church.

6. Clear the Deck

No matter how solid a small-group system is, it will never succeed unless interferences are taken out first. If small groups are at the bottom of a long list of ministry options, they will lose every time. People in your church have only so many hours to give to the church. At least one of those hours is dedicated to the Sunday morning service. Another hour is ideally given in serving somewhere within church. That leaves one more opportunity for church members to give up every week. If offered to them they will take seemingly easier options:

- A midweek service
- A men's ministry meeting
- A women's ministry meeting
- A family ministry event
- A weekly prayer meeting
- A single's ministry event

As individual items, all of these events are good things. But if you really want people to commit to doing life together in challenging small groups, the deck has to be cleared.

Instead of a full-blown men's ministry, consider starting a men's midsize group built on small-group ideals.

Instead of a weekly prayer meeting at the church, craft a message series around the power of prayer and turn it into an all-church study for small groups. I guarantee you will have better participation as well as a lot more people praying in your church.

Clear the deck on the weekends when groups are being launched. Make community the main focus for the message and the logistics for joining a small group the only announcement from the stage. Take out any distractions that would keep people from focusing on groups.

7. Don't Be Afraid to Experiment

A clean slate gives you opportunities to try out different ideas for getting people into community. Not all of them will work the first time, but that is okay. Every time you attempt something new, it gives you metrics to tweak and get better at the next time.

Our first connection event was a complete disaster, but we went back to the white board and adjusted various elements and approaches until it was a success.

Our first attempt at a coaching system did not function as we thought it should, but the results taught us what could work even better.

Poor attendance at large-group trainings forced us to experiment with online options that led to better quality overall.

Don't be afraid try new kinds of groups, different types of training, or different styles of leadership. You will never know what works for your church until you put it into action. One thing, however, is certain: there is no single system that works perfectly for every church. There are proven concepts and principles you can lean on, but every church is unique. Experiment!

Think It Over

- What needs to be blown up in your current groups system?
- What do you consider to be a win for your small groups?
- Who is the champion for groups at your church? If it is not the senior leader, why not?
- Are you putting enough into the budget for the future of groups?
- What do you need to clear away for groups to be successful?
- If nothing were impossible, what would you attempt with groups? Dream big!

5

Search for Leadership

Leadership is not about titles, positions or
flowcharts. It is about one life influencing another.
—John C. Maxwell, *The 21 Irrefutable Laws of Leadership*

Have you ever heard or said, "We just cannot find enough leaders"?
I'm willing to bet nearly all of us have. One of the most difficult
aspects of building an effective small-groups ministry is finding,
recruiting, and training enough leaders to keep up with growth. As
soon as we feel we're in a good place and can finally catch our breath
a little, it's time for another semester and groups push. The ministry
cycle never ends, and neither does the need for solid leaders who hope-
fully won't take their groups off the deep end.

That uncertainty of small-group leadership keeps a lot of pastors from completely releasing groups in their churches. What if bad theology is being taught? What if a popular leader goes rogue and decides to start a new church with his small group? What if a leader attends only group and never shows up on Sunday mornings? The release necessitated with leadership roles is almost as daunting as trying to recruit leaders, but if we let the fear of the unknown trip us up, then great leaders will never step up.

Recruiting

The critical question to start with before you start recruiting leaders is this: How high should I set the bar? Set the leadership bar too high, and you'll always struggle to find leaders. Set the bar too low, and you risk letting your groups collapse because of poor leadership. Further compounding the problem is that you need different levels of leadership within a single system.

There are certain types of groups that require a high bar for leadership. A discipleship-intensive group—like our spiritual leadership group at Cross Point—needs a spiritually mature leader. It would not work to take brand-new Christ followers and task them with teaching systematic theology. Similarly, I would never ask someone in the middle of a recovery group to take leadership of our celebrate-recovery groups. If we set the bar too low for those types of groups, we are not only hurting the church but also setting up the leaders for failure.

However, most churches fall short in recruiting leaders by setting the bar too high across the board. If you require your leaders to jump through a lot of hoops before actually leading a group, you are limiting the ultimate reach of your groups. You might risk having a few groups go south occasionally, but the reward of seeing potential leadership realized in people is worth it.

When Jesus called his first disciples, he didn't look to the established leaders around him. He chose ordinary, uneducated fishermen with big hearts. Jesus knew he could teach knowledge but not passion. If Jesus was willing to turn over the future of the entire church to these guys, we should be okay with releasing our developing leaders to guide our groups.

Dan and his wife, Sarah, were in one of our first groups at Seacoast Church in Greenville. They had been attending the church for just a few months when they decided to join our married couples small group. I quickly saw by the way Dan interacted with the group that he had a huge heart for people. So I asked him if he would facilitate the next group meeting while I was out of town. He hesitated and asked if he and Sarah could sit down with my wife, Jenny, and me before committing.

He shared with us his story of spending time in prison before coming to Christ several years ago. Even though he had completely turned his life around and was now helping with a prison ministry, he was not sure if he was qualified to lead a small group in our church. I assured him he was and hoped he'd lead the group while I was away.

A couple of years later, Dan and Sarah were not only leading their own married couples group but also leading the entire small-groups ministry. If our bar for leadership had been set too high, this would never have happened.

Setting the bar low for leadership creates a lot of opportunities for your church such as these:

- Potential leaders like Dan have a path to leadership.
- You can exponentially expand the number of small groups.
- Your groups have the ability to reach the fringes of the church.
- Small groups can become the new front door for the church.

Host Groups

We have continued to look for low commitment–low risk opportunities for lowering the bar on leadership at Cross Point. The best path for us is through our *host groups strategy*. Three weeks before the all-church campaign, our pastor makes a push from the stage for people to step up and commit to hosting a group for the six weeks during our all-church campaign. We encourage our new hosts to populate their groups with their friends, family, and neighbors. The commitment is low at only six weeks, and focusing on people outside of the church lessens the risk.

We have two levels of host leadership. The entry-level host can be anyone willing to open up their home and invite people they know to attend the group. When they volunteer to host, we give them their curriculum and training on a DVD as part of a host packet in exchange for their information. Our groups directors and coaches will check in with them during the campaign to see how it's going, but we will not send people to their group or include it on our website's list of options. Essentially, a person who does not know Christ could host a group—and they have.

The second level of host makes the same commitment to host a group for the six weeks of the campaign, but they want us to help them fill their group by including them in the connection event and list them on the website. We require this level of host to schedule an interview with the corresponding groups director. At this level of leadership, there are still not a lot of requirements, but we want to make sure we know who we are sending people to.

Leadership Rally

All of our leaders and hosts are then invited to a precampaign rally at one of our campuses. At these rallies we try to accomplish four things in two hours:

- *Inspiration:* We want our leaders and hosts to go into a new semester of group life with excitement and anticipation for what God is going to do in and through their groups. We always invite our senior pastor to share his vision for community at Cross Point, because there is nothing better than hearing *why* from the senior leader.
- *Information:* The leadership rallies give us the opportunity to share anything new first with our leaders and hosts. We will normally give a preview of the curriculum for the all-church study that night and also any new tools we are working on for our groups. We unveiled our curriculum menu at our most recent rally. We also give each groups director time at the end of the night to go over campus-specific information with their leaders and hosts.
- *Training:* Although most of our leader and host training is accomplished online or on a DVD, we always incorporate

some large-group training as a part of the evening. We try to be creative and change it each time. One of our most successful training segments was a panel of seasoned leaders who took questions from the audience and answered how they have handled various situations within their groups.

• *Fun:* With everything we do on that night, ultimately, we want it to be fun. If it's just a night of information, no one will want to come back. One year we hired a game show company to stage a version of *Family Feud,* with leaders from each campus competing as the families would in the TV show format. Along with the usual trivia questions (for example, name a sandwich that tastes great on a roll), we sprinkled in popular small-group practices (name the most popular way to handle someone who talks too much during group). It was a fun way to entertain while also sneaking in a small amount of training.

Each segment of the evening is no longer than twenty minutes, and the evening is always accompanied by a meal. We have discovered that group leaders like to eat well. Our leader and host rallies have become a key component of our recruiting strategy.

Training

Our training for leaders takes a multifaceted approach. The large-group training takes place during our precampaign leader and host rallies, where we hit on best practices for successful small-group leaders. This is where we tackle questions like "How do you handle child care for your group?" We can give ideas, but it helps to hear from other leaders who are working through similar issues. We will also bring in a small-groups expert from the outside to give a different perspective.

As a multisite church, we have discovered that trying to get leaders to come to one location for a series of ongoing training sessions is almost impossible. In order to get maximum participation, we decided to produce as-needed training online. This allows leaders to complete the training at their own pace in their home. After a leader has completed a couple of online modules, their groups director or coach will schedule a quick check-in (usually on a Sunday after the service) to answer questions and make sure they are moving through the training at a good pace. My friend Mac refers to this as "high tech–high touch."

Version 1.0 of our online training was through an online survey website that allowed us to embed videos into the surveys. There are now great options available for churches to not only host their own training videos but also to use canned training modules from some of the best leaders in the country. A few of our online training modules include:

- *Why community?* In this section, our senior pastor shares his heart for why being a part of a biblical community is key to sustained life change and spiritual growth.
- *What does healthy community look like?* In this training module, we paint a picture of what a healthy small group should be doing.
- *A confident leader:* In this module, we share tips for leaders to be more confident in leading their groups.

- *Groups on mission:* For this module, we help groups see how they can move beyond the curriculum and be the hands and feet of Jesus.
- *Leading discussions:* In this practical training, we give tips on facilitating a great discussion that has a finish line.

Putting our basic training online has a lot of upsides to it. There has been higher participation, new leaders can start at any time, there is flexibility in changing it, and so forth. But there are also a few downsides. When we first started our online offerings, we expected leaders to move through the training without deadlines, but a lot of them started modules and never finished them. We now require a meeting with their groups director to talk over what they are learning as they go. This helps motivate the leaders to get through the modules before consulting with the director. But we don't require a leader to finish the training before they start their group. We only ask they progress through the training during the semester. We have found that most of the questions they might normally ask are answered somewhere in the training.

Our training for hosts is much shorter and is contained on a DVD in the host packet they receive when they sign up before a campaign. We purposely kept it to two- to three-minute segments so as not to overwhelm them but to help them with the basics of hosting a group for the six-week campaign. The training topics consist of:

- What is a host?
- How do I fill my group?
- What does a group meeting look like?

- How do I facilitate a discussion?
- What do we do after this study?

Instead of having the staff lead the training, each session is taught by a seasoned group leader. Their personal stories of successes and failures help potential hosts believe they can handle the six-week commitment.

During week three of the all-church study, a coach or director will check in with the hosts and see if they are still open to continuing their group for another six weeks. We will again provide curriculum and get them started with online training. Around 80 percent of our new host groups choose to continue, and a majority of those eventually become a full community group.

When we started small groups from nothing at my campus in Greenville, I took a handful of potential leaders from our core group through an eight-week turbo training group. The purpose of this group was to prepare these leaders for launching groups at the same time the campus launched. Each week I walked the group members through different aspects of leading, and each member had an opportunity to prepare and facilitate a discussion. Because of this turbo group, we were able to launch five successful small groups on the first day our groups went into action.

Retaining

Recruiting and training new leaders is essential to starting new groups, but if you don't retain the leaders you have, you'll find yourself in an endless cycle of never keeping up. We expect a lot from our small-group leaders and hosts. We have commissioned them to pastor a group of people in our church while simultaneously holding down a full-time job and leading a family. Some burnout is inevitable, but there are a few things we can do as church leaders to help our group leaders stay in the game as long as possible:

- *Allow them to take breaks:* We give our leaders permission to not have regular meetings with their groups during the summer and the winter holiday months. We encourage them to do occasional activities outside of their group, such as serving on a mission trip or getting together for a picnic, and we also suggest they take a break from everything that goes into hosting a weekly group. We find that leaders are reenergized and ready to get started again when they return from a few weeks off.

  It's also healthy to allow group leaders to occasionally take a semester off from leading. There are seasons of life that necessitate taking a step back and renewing before reengaging in ministry. Even Jesus took periodic breaks during his three years of ministry. We should allow our leaders to do the same.

- *Give regular appreciation:* We do this on a large scale for our leaders twice a year. We throw a party every August for all of our leaders at one location, and each campus sponsors its own celebration every January. We also encourage all our directors and coaches to be creative and appreciate their leaders in smaller ways throughout the year. This could be a personalized note of thanks or a Starbucks gift card for just being awesome. If small-group leaders feel like the church leadership never acknowledges them, they will move on to somewhere that will.

- *Tell their stories:* Nothing renews passion more than hearing stories of life change. We gather with the entire church staff every Tuesday for lunch, and the first thing we do is share ministry stories from the past week. It is inevitable that someone will tear up as they share something amazing God has done in a person's life that week. These thirty to forty minutes are by far the best part of the workweek for me. I cannot wait to get back into the fray after hearing stories of how God is working in our church. It's the same with our small-group leaders. The more they hear about why what they do matters, the more committed they are to making a difference. We love to collect the stories, but we need to always remember to share them with our leaders.

- *Give them ongoing training:* Offering more in-depth training tells a leader that you believe in them and they are capable of bigger things. This could be through one-on-one mentoring, an occasional online module for a new skill, or offering a new book to read together. Growing leaders are never finished learning. Continue to look for new ways to invest in helping them be better at what they do.

Promoting

A small-group system is a natural pipeline for leadership in your church. If you are looking for future staff members, start with the people who have made their way through the ranks in your groups. Each step of the pipeline provides opportunities to acquire and demonstrate new levels of leadership. It's up to us to provide the space and training for them to move through those levels.

It starts with training leaders to share the load of leadership with their small-group members. Most groups need a food preparer, a prayer request taker, a communications director, a fun outing finder, and so on. While some of these roles may seem small, and it would be much easier for the leader to just take care of them, it gives new small-group attenders a chance to show their leadership potential. If they can be consistent with their designated role within the group, it might be time to move them to the next level as a small-group apprentice.

The role of apprentice can be a formal designation in the system or it can be an organic move. I didn't crown Dan as my official apprentice in my first group, but I occasionally trusted him to facilitate the discussions. After he had facilitated a group meeting, we would touch base and talk about how it had gone. We teach the five steps for building up apprentices as outlined in Dave and Jon Ferguson's book, *Exponential*.[1]

Step 1: I do. You watch. We talk.

Step 2: I do. You help. We talk.

Step 3: You do. I help. We talk.

Step 4: You do. I watch. We talk.

Step 5: You do. Someone else watches.

The key to promoting an apprentice is slowly releasing the reins of leadership until the apprentice is prepared for doing it on her own. This process eventually led to Dan and his wife starting their own small group as leaders.

The responsibility of leading a small group may be the top level in the pipeline for most leaders, but a few will be able and willing to do more. Adding a coaching tier helps not only to provide soul care for other group leaders but also to give potential future staff members a chance to prove themselves capable of leading at that level. Keep in mind that your coaches will need different skills and training to successfully make the turn from small-group leader to coach. A common error at this level is assuming that what made them an effective group leader will automatically translate to the next area of responsibility. Look for these characteristics in an effective coach:

- *Good listener:* The first priority for a small-groups coach is to listen to the leaders and hosts in his care. Just talking it out with someone else can solve most issues that come up in groups. A coach does not have to feel like she has all the answers to every question.
- *Seasoned groups leader:* The same issues tend to come up over and over within small groups. A coach who has led groups for a few seasons will most likely have dealt with the issues that will show up in a new group. She can lean on that experience as she guides a new leader or host.
- *Good communicator:* Nothing is more frustrating to a new leader than a coach or director who doesn't communicate well with him. Before committing to coaching

for a semester, a potential coach should make sure that his schedule allows him time to adequately stay in touch with his leaders. If there is a desperate text sent in the midst of a crisis, a coach should be on top of the response.

- *Leader of leaders:* In his book *The Five Levels of Leadership,* John Maxwell outlines five different levels of leadership and how they work to attract other leaders.[2] He says that level 3 leaders will attract and retain level 1 and level 2 leaders. Level 4 leaders will retain level 3 and level 2 leaders, and level 5 leaders will retain level 4 and level 3 leaders. You want to go after level 4 and level 5 leaders to be coaches. They will raise the level of leadership throughout your system.

- *Prayer warrior:* A small-groups coach should be driven to her knees for the needs of the leaders she coaches. The final question for every coaching conversation should be "How can I pray for you?" Once someone has proven herself as an effective coach, she may be ready to move up to being responsible for a bigger piece of the system or the whole ministry at a staff level. For us at Cross Point, this level of the pipeline is a groups director. Our directors have oversight for small groups at the campus level. This ranges from a high-capacity volunteer overseeing twenty groups to a full-time director responsible for over two hundred groups. A mistake we made at this level was seeing the need and putting someone in this position before they had proven themselves at the other levels of the pipeline. You might have a potential leader who is willing to skip to the top, but their lack of experience and skills will eventually catch up with them. Taking the necessary time to develop leaders through the process will help ensure success for the long term.

A driven leader is more likely to stick with the program if he has the potential of being promoted through the levels of the system. Build into the system clear and obvious steps for him to take. How does a small-group member start functioning as an apprentice? Is it easy for apprentices to start their own group? Do you have training in place for a leader to take the next step as a coach? Are you looking first within your system for your next staff members?

Releasing

A few senior pastors worry that their small groups will eventually leave and start their own churches if the pastors give up complete control. Because of this fear, they never loosen their grip on the potential of groups in the community.

The way we will eventually reach our cities with the gospel of Jesus is by commissioning our leaders as pastors and missionaries in their communities. The tighter we hold on to control, the less effective our small groups will be. Great leaders will eventually do it with or without us, so why not recognize the potential and resource them with what we have been given?

A highly functioning small-groups system can be a very effective way to plant a new church. If a gifted leader eventually feels the call to start a church, stand behind him and give him enough funding and support to get the dream off of the ground. So many church planters are currently struggling because their home church could not see beyond the immediate situation to the greater kingdom. Connected small groups in a community are already planting these seeds needed for a new church to start strong:

- They are already inviting their neighbors and friends to experience biblical community.
- They are already connected to the local school system.
- They are the business leaders of the area.

Small groups are also an effective way to start a new campus. You may have a small-group leader who is highly relational but not gifted as a weekly communicator. He has started several successful groups and is now coaching a network of thriving groups that are working together. Instead of doing a national search for your next campus pastor, why not walk alongside this leader and release him to do what he is already doing? Those leaders may not have seminary degrees, but they have already proven themselves ready to be commissioned as campus pastors in your church.

In the book *Multi-Site Church Revolution*, my brother Geoff tells the story of how one of our most successful small-groups leaders and coaches at Seacoast Church became our first nonstaff hire as a campus pastor:

By the time Seacoast was ready to open its sixth campus, we (Geoff) knew we couldn't afford to drain any more talent from the existing staff, so we turned to our small-group system to find our next campus pastor. Phil Strange was the ideal candidate. Phil had committed his life to Christ at Seacoast several years earlier. His first place of ministry had been working in the parking ministry on the weekends. He soon started volunteering with his wife, Sherry, in the nursery. Eventually someone invited Phil and Sherry to attend their small group, and Phil became the worship leader because he was the one who knew how to play the guitar. When the group divided, Phil and Sherry led the new group, and a few months later, they were asked to coach several group leaders. Phil had never been to seminary, had never given a sermon, had never performed a wedding, baptism, or funeral, but he was the ideal candidate for a campus pastor. Beyond meeting the biblical qualifications for an elder, Phil was a proven leader, he had the Seacoast DNA, and the culture was already engrained in him. All he needed was a little on-the-job training, some basic theological and pastoral instruction, and a lot if support. His campus launched three months after he came on staff and grew to over 500 people within the first year.[3]

Over ten years later, Phil is still the campus pastor, and his campus is now reaching thousands every weekend. There are small-group leaders like Phil in your church who are just waiting to be commissioned to launch that next campus or start the next church. Remember that God will equip the called. All you have to do is provide the means and runway for success.

Think It Over

- Do you currently have enough leaders to handle your growth?
- Where are you looking for most of your leaders?

- Do you need to consider lowering the bar for leadership?
- What kind of training do you offer your leaders? Should you move some of it online to reach more potential leaders?
- How well are you keeping your leaders? Are they free to take breaks?
- Do you have a clearly defined leadership pipeline for leaders to follow?
- Was your last staff hire an effective small-group leader from within your system? Why or why not?

6

Connecting the Crowd

We have all known the long loneliness and
we have learned that the only solution is love
and that love comes with community.
—Dorothy Day, *The Long Loneliness*

You may have designed the best small-groups system you possibly could. You may have handpicked, mentored, and trained the brightest leaders in your church. But none of it matters if the majority of the people in your church never get connected to a group. We can spend so much time and efforts designing the structure and then assume people will just show up.

No matter how difficult you make the entry points, you can count on a core of 20 percent at least giving it a try. They are so committed to the church and the vision that they will fight through any barriers to be in a group. Make it a little easier to join a group and you might get 10 to 15 percent more to give it a go. But so many churches never get past the 50 percent barrier because it takes different approaches to move beyond the core to the crowd. You cannot have one entry point and expect to reach the final 50 percent.

New Groups

The best strategy for reaching new people is starting new groups. New people may attend an existing group once, but most of them will not continue to attend, especially if they were not invited by someone already in the group and were either placed in the group by a staff member or chose it themselves from a menu of groups on the website. No matter how open and friendly a group may be to new people, new-comers are walking onto an uneven playing field. If you ever had to move and change schools when you were growing up, you know what that feeling is like. There is already history and relationships formed within the group, and trying to catch up with everyone else takes more effort than most people are willing to give to a group. Open groups sound like a great strategy, but they just don't work.

Our family struggled to make new relationships when we first moved to Nashville. It seemed as if everyone we met had already filled their relationship quotas. To better connect to our community, we decided to start a small group after a couple of months and open it up to anyone. What we discovered were eight other couples who were struggling just like us. Most of them had just moved to the area and were experiencing the same kind of isolation we were. Five years later, those same couples are still some of our closest friends. We would never have had those life experiences if we had not made the decision to start a new group and see what happens.

Starting a new group levels the playing field for everyone. The expectations for relationships have not been established yet. There is a mutual feeling of "we are all in this together, so let's see if we can make this work."

We discovered how well this could work at Cross Point when we launched a midsize group for young adults. Nashville is filled with young professionals who have moved here to chase a dream. Most of them are not connected into community and are hungry for relationships. After attempting to connect as many young professionals as we could into existing groups, we realized we needed to utilize the strategy of starting new groups to keep up with the demand. A midsize group that met on campus allowed us to grow exponentially and also provided a constant source of new small groups. Two to three new groups were being formed every month in response to the flow of new people.

Our first question to someone requesting a group is, "Would you be interested in starting a group?" Not everyone will be ready to start a new group, but we want to at least start the conversation. So many people respond, "I hadn't thought about starting a group, but please tell me more about it." Just giving the option changes the mentality from consumer to contributor. They are also more likely to stick in community if the responsibility of forming that community is on them. They are no longer just kicking the tires but actually helping to build the car.

All-Church Campaigns

An effective way to start several new groups at one time is by aligning your church around the same topic once or twice a year. We schedule campaigns for our major growth seasons in February and September. Doing an all-church study brings several benefits:

- All of our groups are speaking the same language for six weeks. With a modified, free-market system, it's rare that everyone in our church is on the same page. You can feel the buzz on Sundays when everyone is headed in the same direction.
- We discover new leaders who would have never stepped up any other way. The push to host a group for the campaign forces people to step out of their comfort zone and contribute.
- It reenergizes our current leaders. Some of our leaders need a reason to get excited about leading a group again. The excitement of a campaign brings new life to their groups.
- It forces our groups staff to be creative. Building an interactive study around our pastor's messages is not always easy. The process makes us think through every aspect of group life and how we can best set up our leaders and hosts for success.
- It realigns our leaders and staff with the heart of our pastor. It's easy to drift away from the vision of the church over time. An all-church study helps bring us back to the core values of who we are as a church. We are walking in lockstep with our senior leader.

Our pastor typically plans out his message series three to four months ahead of time, so I make sure to schedule some time with him in October and June to see where he is leaning on those campaign weeks. Occasionally he will have a solid direction, and we will build off that, but a lot of the time he is open to ideas and we are able to brainstorm together on what might work best for groups and the congregation.

Our most successful campaigns have resulted from our planning far enough in advance, with enough time to design our curriculum and put the pastor in the small groups' living rooms on video. We discovered that people will buy into a study much quicker when it's our teaching pastor setting up the discussion each week. We keep the introductory videos short (eight to ten minutes), and use them as a handoff to the facilitator for the big idea of the session. One of our studies was based completely online to keep printing and duplicating costs down. It also helps when the pastor releases a book and someone else does the heavy lifting of designing the study and shooting videos for us.

It doesn't always work out to build your own curriculum for the campaign. We either do not have enough time to do it the way we would like or we can find something on the shelf that fits perfectly with where the pastor wants to go with the message series. A few years ago, our pastor wanted to focus on the idea of God's love. Bob Goff's book *Love Does*[2] had just been released, and we thought it would be perfect to build a curriculum around it for the series. After a few weeks of struggling to make the book work for us as a small-group study, we discovered that Saddleback Church's 40 Days of Love campaign study was a much better fit. It became one of our most successful all-church campaigns ever.

With our most recent campaign, as of this writing, we were able to start over two hundred new groups. Not all of those groups will continue after the initial six-week study, but even if only half of them do, that is one hundred more groups than we had before the campaign started. I will take that success ratio every time.

On- and Off-Ramps

I grew up in East Texas, which means when we wanted to vacation on a beach (where you could actually see what was in the water around you), we would head to Florida. On our way to those white-sand beaches, just before the swamps of Louisiana, there was a sign on the interstate that advertised the next exit as being twenty-five miles ahead. I remember seeing that sign as a kid and immediately panicking as I quickly thought through every drink and snack I had consumed since the last rest stop. Those were always the longest twenty-five miles in my life because of the thought of no off-ramps that offered relief.

If we expect our people to have a panic-free experience with group life, we have to design easy and obvious on- and off-ramps in community. What are the obstacles that keep people from getting into and out of groups? Are they afraid to commit because it feels like a lifetime, no-way-out contract?

Semesters

A few years ago we decided to move to a semester format for our groups calendar. We now run three semesters through the year. Our fall semester kicks off in late August and runs through November. The winter semester starts in late January and goes to Easter. And the spring semester launches two weeks after Easter and runs through June.

The beginning of each semester gives us a natural place to start new groups with a lot of momentum. If new members come to our church during the middle of a semester, it's only a few weeks until we are starting a new batch of groups for them to join. Defining the end of semesters reassures people that there will be an opportunity to step out of a group without feeling guilty. It also gives our leaders a chance to catch their breath before taking on another season.

Although we give our leaders a break from the burden of leading a weekly small-group meeting during the summer, we encourage them to stay connected as a group by hosting a neighborhood block party, participating in a local or global missions opportunity, and doing something fun together as a group. Just like we don't believe church is all about the weekend, community is not all about the study. It's healthy for a group to step out of their normal routine for a couple of months to do something different.

Lobby Presence

One of my favorite things to do while on vacation is attend church. That seems really odd coming from someone who makes a living by working for a church, but I am a self-proclaimed church junky. I love discovering how other churches are successfully reaching people for Christ. It also gives me a chance to just worship. Whenever I am at my home church, I am constantly thinking through everything around me instead of focusing on what God wants to say to me that morning.

I am consistently amazed at how difficult churches can make it for a new person to discover how to plug into community at their church. It's usually not too difficult to find out where to drop off my kids. The coffee and doughnuts are featured prominently. I can follow the crowd into the main auditorium. But my path to being in a small group is nowhere to be found.

If the best way to shut the back door to your church is to get people plugged into community as soon as possible, then why wouldn't you make that path obvious to visitors to your church? Even if your system allows people to join groups only at certain times of the year, there should be a designated spot in the lobby to tell them the why and how behind your assimilation strategy.

The volunteers in charge of that space should be equipped with the most recent information for how groups work at the church. There is nothing more frustrating for a visitor than approaching an information desk at the church and discovering that the person on the other side can't answer his questions or has out-of-date information for the ministry. If a volunteer does not immediately know the answer, she should at least know the right staff member to ask.

Online Options

When I first came to Cross Point, we were still listing all of our groups in a printed magazine format. This required the groups staff to track down all the information from leaders and make sure it was all as accurate as possible before going to print. If some of the information was wrong or had changed after the print date, it was too late to do anything about it. The cost of printing devoured most of our small-groups annual budget, so we couldn't afford to continually update and reprint the information. Offering book listings also forced people to be physically present at church when the books were handed out on a Sunday. If they missed that day, most of the groups would be already closed by the time they could get the information.

Moving all of our group listings online gave us several benefits:

- *Lower cost:* We were able to take the money we were spending on printing and use it to produce our own curriculum for all-church campaigns. It also freed up money for coffees and lunches with our leaders.
- *Flexibility:* We never worry about a group changing their information at the last minute. We can add and subtract groups from the website at any point during the semester. We can guarantee new people that the groups represented on the website are open to join at any time.
- *Always available:* People no longer have to be present at church to get a listing of available groups. They don't even have to attend our church before joining a small group.
- *Expected:* In today's online world, if the information cannot be found quickly on a mobile phone, it doesn't exist. When I'm looking for information on a new restaurant, I don't pull out the yellow pages and give them a call. I open an app on my smartphone. Not only does the information for groups need to be online, but it cannot be buried deep in the website. One or two clicks are the limit people will exert to find anything.

The downside to putting groups online is it can depersonalize the process. Instead of having someone with the church hand off a newcomer to a group leader, they can pick a group from a generic list.

We try to combat this by not putting the leader's information on the online listing but having the first contact come from one of our staff of group directors. This helps to ensure that the group will be a good fit, and a newcomer has someone to check with if the group leader doesn't get back with them.

Stage Time

For groups to become a cultural norm in a church, they have to be talked about as much as possible. In an episode of *Seinfeld*, George decided the only way he could get a girl to show any interest in him was by getting his name stuck in her head like a commercial jingle. By the end of the episode, she caught herself singing his name to the tune of "Buy Mennen" without even thinking.[2]

People need to leave church every Sunday singing the words "join a group" in their head. This is accomplished not just through making a small-groups announcement every week, because people start to tune out the same announcements after a while, but by becoming a natural part of the language from the stage. The senior pastor casually mentions something that happened in his group the past week during his message. The person doing the welcome section of the service talks about how the best way for people to connect to the heart of the church is through joining a small group. The service closing always includes logistics for how to investigate joining a group. After a few months of this, people who are not connected to a group start to feel like they are missing out on something.

When it is time to make specific announcements about groups, people respond best to stories, not information. Apple commercials make you want to buy an overpriced gizmo not by telling you all of the details of its processing power but through stories of how it made people's lives better. You want to buy a Harley-Davidson motorcycle because the advertisements show a biker leaning into a curve on a beautiful day in the mountains. Never mind that you live nowhere near a mountain, you need to have that life. Leadership author and guru Simon Sinek says in the TED Talk based on his book *Start with Why*, "People don't buy what you do, they buy why you do it."[3] Stories of life-change through the power of community are why people will give small groups a go.

Look for those stories throughout the year, and store them for when you can use them during a groups push. Put the stories on video to be shown at the end of the service. At Cross Point, we have also used them in social media campaigns leading up to a semester kickoff. Each day is a different snapshot of a story on Facebook, Twitter, and Instagram. Instead of producing the normal program or bulletin on that Sunday, put two or three stories and a QR code to your groups sign-up website in it.

It's also vital on those semester kickoff Sundays that how to join a small group is the *only* announcement. If you send people out of the building with too many messages, small groups will get lost in the mix. Doing this will take discipline and sacrifice from the other ministries in the church, but if you truly believe that life change happens best within the context of community, then small groups should be the only focus for the day.

Connection Events

Our sign-up to show-up percentage at Cross Point went from around 40 percent to 80 percent after implementing our connection event strategy. Before we did this, our campuses would host a typical small-groups fair on semester kickoff Sundays. Each campus would have a few leaders available in the lobby for people to meet after the service, and then they could decide if they wanted to sign up for a group. We included a sign-up card in the worship program if they'd rather fill it out and drop it in the offering.

Our senior pastor, however, is amazing when it comes to selling the vision of community for our church, so our sign-up numbers were typically extremely high. But we discovered that large sign-ups did not always equate to people actually showing up for groups. After they had a chance to go home and think about it, the fear of the unknown caused them to stay home. We needed something stickier.

What if we could eliminate the biggest imagined fears of being in a small group? We looked at what North Point Community Church in Atlanta was doing with their group link events and similar strategies at Saddleback Church, and we eventually created a version that we thought would work in our culture.

After the pastor gives the vision for small groups, we invite anyone who is interested in exploring groups further to join us for a connect event that week. Each night of the week is tailored for group leaders and hosts who will be meeting on that particular night for the next six weeks. If someone thinks a group meeting on Monday nights might work best for them, they could come to the event on

Monday. If Wednesdays worked better for others, they could come on Wednesday night. And so on.

At the event, we set up round tables throughout the room with colored balloons representing the type of group and information about where the groups would meet. As each person enters the room, they are greeted by a small-groups coach or director and handed a menu with a diagram of the room with a color key for the balloons (red = men's group, pink = women's group, green = married couples, etc.). After our first attempt, we discovered there was no difference between light green balloons and dark green balloons. We're pretty sure a few married couples accidently joined some single-adult groups that semester.

The menu also includes three questions to think about as the newcomers go about choosing a group:

- What day/time of week works best for you?
- Who do you want to connect with?
- Where do you live?

Coaches and directors are there to be a guide to help the new-comers find the right table and answer any additional questions they might have. We structure the evening as much as possible to be like a group meeting. We give them twenty minutes at the beginning to grab some snacks and get to know the people around their table. A stage host then welcomes everyone and gives the overall agenda for the next ninety minutes. We've discovered it's important to keep to your word and begin and end on time. And we want to model for the attenders what we expect from our leaders and hosts at their own groups.

If we are launching our all-church study that week, we start with the introductory video for week one and walk the groups through four rounds of questions from the study. Each round builds on the last and allows the group to gradually become more open as the night progresses. After the last round of questions, the stage host thanks everyone for coming and explains how they have just experienced what it is like to be in a community group at Cross Point.

All of the typical fears—Who will be in my group? What will we talk about for two hours?—have been answered that night. All that is left to do is to decide the location and time your group will meet for the next six weeks. The host then instructs everyone to turn their menu over, which has a place for the newcomers to write down their contact information for the leader or host and a tear-off portion to record the details about the group. If a table doesn't already have a designated leader or a host, we ask them to decide who could host the group and/or facilitate discussion for the next six weeks.

Before we dismiss everyone, we ask the newly chosen hosts to stick around for a few minutes so we can get their information and give them a host packet and the curriculum for the study. All brand-new hosts are given the curriculum for an all-church study for free, because we want to eliminate as many barriers to hosting a group as possible. Veteran group leaders are able to purchase the curriculum at reduced prices.

The leaders and hosts then follow up the next day with an e-mail reminding everyone at their table of the details for the next group meeting. If someone misses the connection event but still wants to join a group, they have an opportunity the next couple of weeks to join one through connection cards that we stuff in the Sunday programs or by choosing a group from our online listings.

The New Front Door

Connection events have proven to be the best strategy for getting people *within* our church into a small group, but if we are going to make a serious dent in our communities, small groups have to become a new entry point for the church. I love the *invest and invite* strategy that North Point Church in Atlanta has taught their people for inviting their unchurched friends to church. But how much stickier would the invite be if the investment was through an invitation to be a part of a small group first?

- They will have already been exposed to the pastor's teachings through the videos from the all-church study.
- There is built-in follow-up through the group meetings.
- There is no rush to get them there on a Sunday.
- It starts and continues with relationship.

The more we move away from the mentality of "the weekend is everything," the better chance we have to reach entire cities. Don't get me wrong, weekend services are important, but they cannot be the only tool in the evangelism toolbox. It's natural to rely on Sundays, because drawing a large crowd is fairly easy, but creating and nurturing relationships through groups is more difficult.

Flipping the paradigm will take a concerted effort from the entire church and staff. If 90 percent of your outreach budget goes solely toward putting on a Sunday morning service, it might be time to reexamine your priorities. Small groups meeting in homes and inviting their neighbors to join them give us the best chance to reach the

40 percent who would never walk into our churches. Resource allocations should reflect how important they are to the vision of the gospel.

Think It Over

- What is your current strategy for bringing new people into community? Is it effective?
- How difficult is it to start new groups in your church?
- Do you currently offer all-church studies for your groups? If not, why not?
- What are your on- and off-ramps for people to get into groups? Are they easy to take?
- How common is it for people on stage to talk about groups in your church?
- Where are small groups on your church's priority list? Are they functioning as a front door for people?

7

Setting Expectations

The pessimist complains about the
wind; the optimist expects it to change;
the realist adjusts the sails.
—William Arthur Ward

Before you ask anyone to lead or host a group at your church, you have
to ask the following question: What does an effective small group at
our church look like? A lot of group systems fail because there were
no clear expectations set from the beginning. If leaders are not given a
clear picture of what a successful group looks like, there will be frus-
tration on both sides. You're helping set up a leader to win by giving
clear guardrails for her to work within.

Does the Parking Team Count?

One of the initial decisions you have to make for your groups system is what constitutes an official small group at your church. Most churches technically already have small groups. You probably have a guest experience group that greets people at the doors on Sundays or serves coffee. You may have a parking group that gathers early on Sundays to pray before heading out to help people find parking spaces. You may also have a choir group, a kids ministry volunteer group, a worship team group, a facilities group, a security team group, and a variety of other ministry group possibilities. It would be easy to declare all of these ministry teams to be small groups, but they may or may not be meeting the expectations of spiritual formation in your church.

Before you declare your usher team an official small group in your system, examine all of your groups with these questions:

- *What is the goal?* Ministry groups may fill the purpose of serving, but if your goal for groups is making disciples, that is only one piece of the puzzle. Start with the end in mind and decide if your groups are designed to get you there.
- *Is there community?* A ministry group may have time to gather for a few minutes before they serve prior to or after a service, but are they experiencing real life-on-life community?
- *What is the content?* Unless a ministry team is also meeting outside of their normal service time, there is probably not enough margin for an in-depth study.
- *What are the core elements?* For us at Cross Point, we ask every group to be balanced in evangelism, community,

and mission. A ministry group can only focus on one or two of those practices at a time.

- *What is the experience?* We have expectations of what someone will experience if they join a small group at Cross Point. Each element is designed to help them take their next steps toward Christ.
- *How do you measure growth?* There is no way to know if your groups are meeting expectations without a way to measure it. An effective small group shows spiritual growth.

Ministry teams are groupings of people but not necessarily groups. Our goal is for small groups to feed people into our ministry teams as they discover their gifts for service in the church.

Singing Is Bad

After you have set your expectations for what an official small group is in your church, you have to make it clear what you expect to take place within those groups.

When my wife and I started our first small group, there was an expectation at our church for groups to have an element of singing together for worship. I was a musician and a worship leader at that time, so each week I would pick out two or three songs and lead them with an acoustic guitar. I would also print out the lyrics so everyone could have something to stare at instead of the person across from you in the circle. If you think men aren't singing during your Sunday morning worship, try forcing them to sing in a small group of twelve people.

I had visions as a worship leader of experiencing deeply moving worship times during which we could feel the power and presence of God in the room. What I got in reality were a few brave souls willing to help me out and a bunch of guys silently praying for it all to be over so they could hit the desserts in the kitchen.

Outside of a worship team small group, I have never experienced singing together as an effective element in a small-group meeting. Worship can also be expressed in a group through prayer, reading God's Word, and moments of solitude together.

So what are the core elements that should be taking place at a small group? Here are a few that we look for in our groups:

- *Food:* You have probably picked up by now that I like to eat—a lot. Not every group has to serve food as part of their meetings, but food can help to knock down barriers to conversation. We encourage every group to start with a meal at an affordable restaurant to encourage open conversation from the beginning.
- *Laughter:* When I visit a small group, I can sense how healthy a group is by how much laughter is in the room. Spiritual formation is not meant to be a somber, boring exercise. (That is saved for seminary! :)) The tone of fun starts with the leader.
- *Study:* A small group without the element of study is a social club. Curriculum does not equal discipleship, but it helps generate the necessary conversations to get there.
- *Dialogue:* Spiritual transformation happens through the questioning of our beliefs and unbeliefs as long as the

truth of God's Word is always the landing place for the discussion.

- *Prayer:* I always regret when I let the discussion bleed into our time for prayer for one another. It's so easy to breeze through a quick prayer at the end to wrap things up on time. Taking time to hear one another's needs is an essential part of group life.

If singing together is your thing, then by all means incorporate it in your program. Otherwise, find the core elements that every group meeting should have and train your leaders to implement them successfully in their groups.

Leave the Teaching to John Ortberg

Most of our new group leaders and hosts are relieved when we let them know through the training that we are not asking them to teach a lesson each week at their small group. All we ask is that they facilitate a conversation around the topic through the questions provided in the curriculum. In fact, we encourage them to talk for less than 30 percent of the time during the discussion. Those inevitable, awkward silences will eventually force group members to engage in dialogue instead of waiting for the leader to always have the answers.

To help our leaders have strong, theologically correct content to use to launch conversations, we lean heavily on DVD-based studies. All of our recommended studies have been previewed by the groups team and given a test run by a few seasoned groups. We feel like DVD-based studies bring several benefits to our groups:

- *We can control the content for the discussions.* Collective ignorance makes for really bad theology. We want the starting material to guide the group in the right direction. They can still occasionally end up in the wrong landing place, but they are much less likely to do so with strong source material.

- *Each week starts with a gifted communicator.* A good teacher can lay the foundation for a great discussion. A bad teacher will shut it down before it can get started. Most of the greatest communicators in the world are engaged in creating curriculum for small groups to use. Why should we not take advantage of it?

- *The best DVD studies come with well-written study guides.* The questions are designed to build on each other to lead the group through different stages of processing. By the end of the evening, they should be equipped to see the world around them a little bit differently than they did before. A facilitator's job is to keep bringing the focus back to where the finish line is for the evening.

- *More studies are becoming available online.* A group no longer has to purchase a DVD and make sure the player is hooked up to the television in the room where the group is gathered. They can either show it from a decent-sized computer screen or stream it through a device like a Roku or an Apple TV. This freedom allows us to produce our own content faster and cheaper than ever before. One of our recent video message studies was completely based online. Our pastor would shoot bonus content for his message on Thursday, and we would upload it to the website by Sunday for our groups to use that week.

There are always a few group leaders who feel the desire to teach rather than facilitate. A couple of years ago, a well-meaning leader approached her campus pastor with the idea of leading her group through a self-written study of eschatology based on the book of Revelation. The campus pastor was also Facebook friends with her and had noticed her recent posts contained extremist views on the end times. It was a difficult conversation but a pretty easy call to discourage her from teaching her own material to the group.

The Last Time I Read a Book Was in College

We discourage our leaders from doing straight-up book studies with their groups. The unfortunate reality, is that most people don't read anymore. Especially guys. There is a good reason why Twitter limited posts to 140 characters. That is about the attention span of most people in our social media–driven world. If a blog post or a news item stretches into more than one scroll down the page, people have already moved on to the next item.

Several years ago I realized that book studies no longer worked with groups when we decided to take our couples group through a quick study of the book *The Prayer of Jabez* by Bruce Wilkinson. If you have read the book, you know it's a quick read. The entire book is ninety-six pages long! As I looked around the room to start the first discussion, not a single guy made eye contact with me. I knew immediately that no one had read the book. They could have finished it in the time most of them took to drive to group, but it didn't happen. If I couldn't convince them to read *The Prayer of Jabez*, my next book study idea of *Mere Christianity* was already dead in the water.

If a group does decide to do a book study, the first part of the discussion is spent catching most of the group up on what they didn't get to read during the week. Some people feel so guilty about not doing the reading, they will make excuses for not making it to group again until the study is over.

Most good Christian books have companion DVD small-group studies. We always suggest to our leaders that they wait to use a book until the study becomes available, usually around six months after the release of the book.

I Understood No Math Would Be Involved . . .

A few expectations we tend to put on our leaders can make it start to feel like they're high school teachers instead of small-group facilitators. It is important to know how many people are actively attending groups, but asking leaders to take weekly attendance is the wrong way to do it.

- Attendance is one more thing for a leader to have to keep up with every week. They are already putting in extra hours to host and facilitate a group.

- The goal of the group can become about numbers. Each week's attendance will fluctuate along with members' schedules. A leader does not need the extra pressure of feeling like a failure on the down weeks.

Instead of working off of weekly attendance numbers, we take periodic snapshots to figure out our percentages. A few weeks into each semester, we ask each group to give us an updated roster of who is actually attending their group. We then contact the people who didn't stick to see if they would like to start a group or try another one. All of this goes into our main church database to form our numbers for the semester.

Our goal is always to create a near friction-free experience for our leaders and hosts. The heavy lifting should always fall on the staff, not the volunteers. We worry about the numbers so they can shepherd their groups.

Couples Groups Do Not Work

Bob and Crystal were a really nice married couple who joined a small group. At the first gathering for the semester at a restaurant, Bob seemed to jell with the guys, and Crystal jumped right in with the other women in their conversations. I was excited about what this new couple would contribute to the group, but the next week I noticed, when it came time for the discussion part of group, Crystal would offer her thoughts, but Bob would always keep quiet. This was the same guy who was completely comfortable talking at the restaurant the week before but now had nothing to add. As this scenario continued for the next few weeks, I also observed that if the other guys contributed to the discussion, their thoughts were mostly superficial.

This is why couples groups will always struggle when it comes to being open and vulnerable. Most men will not open up in front of their spouse. They will talk about work or the game last night, but if there is a chance of vulnerability during the discussion, they yield to their wife every time.

Couples groups can be more effective if the discussion time is split into women and men subgroups. This doesn't have to happen every week, but the group is much more likely to wrestle with the subject matter if they have opportunities to be open with others of their same gender. For complete openness, it's important to stipulate that what is discussed in those subgroups must stay confidential. There is nothing worse than a guy opening up to the other guys and then having something he said brought up later for prayer when the group is back together. He has to know that the other guys in the group respect his openness by keeping some things confidential.

Couples groups can also be more effective when the members are connected to other men's and women's groups. There is openness and accountability in same-sex groups that is not achievable when discussion ensues in a mixed-gender group. While men's and women's ministries are dying off, I believe gender-specific small groups bring much-needed value to the spiritual growth of a person. Here are three reasons to cultivate same-gender groups:

1. *We need natural places to find godly examples and mentors to follow.* Partly because our church is

filled with young single adults, we are constantly getting requests for spiritual mentors. The best space for those relationships to organically develop is in a men's or women's small group.

2. *Transformation can only occur alongside accountability.* For real change to take place in a person's life, he needs a group of brothers to hold him accountable to those changes. He can too easily hide behind his wife in a married couples group.

3. *Same gender groups can be intergenerational.* Most of our small groups are divided by stage of life or location demographics. We have young couples groups, married without kids groups, empty nester groups, and so on. While these groups are important, we are missing something critical when we do not have the influence that older and younger generations can provide. In *A Different Kind of Tribe*, Rick Howerton wrote:

> Young adults need and long for older adults to mentor them. Their heart's desire is for people of age to journey alongside them. They are simply waiting for the church to create a setting of inter-generational people that feels natural and where authenticity is promoted. They not only want to learn life skills, they also want older adults to unveil their mishaps and struggles and tell them what they've learned in the process. No setting meets these expectations better than a healthy intergenerational small group.[1]

I Don't Like Everyone in My Group

A lot of potential leaders shy away from leading a group because of the false belief that they have to be just like the senior pastor to lead. Most successful, growing churches have a charismatic leader at the helm. He is probably very likable and is seen most Sundays in the lobby kissing babies and shaking hands. Of course that's just a small part of the profile. But if we are asking our leaders to pastor a small subset of our church, the natural reaction is that they believe they have to live up to the example set by the staff and pastors on Sunday mornings. They think that to lead a group, they have to always be on and have everyone love them.

But it's impossible for a leader to be relationally close with everyone in her group. It's not even healthy to attempt to nourish that many relationships. Attempting to be everything to everyone will quickly lead to burnout and missed expectations of the group members. Group leaders need to understand that, just as their role is to facilitate focused conversation, they are only responsible for facilitating relationships within the group.

In his book *Organic Community*, Joseph Myers describes the four patterns of belonging that every person can experience:[2]

- *Public belonging:* This is where most small groups are going to start. You share common ground by attending the same church or living in the same neighborhood. There is a natural language among all of the members of the group.
- *Social belonging:* This is the handful of people in the group you are not afraid to ask a favor from. They might

help a group member move to a new house over the week-end. Or it may be a group of guys from the group who own motorcycles and like to ride together a couple of times a month.

- *Personal belonging:* These are relationships that grow out of social connections. You're willing to share a personal prayer need outside of group time with these two or three people. They would be considered close friends.
- *Intimate belonging:* In this space are the one or two best friends who can share the most personal joys and hurts. This level of intimacy may not necessarily live within the context of the group or even the church, but everyone needs it.

Where new small-group leaders struggle under the weight of expectations is when they feel the pressure to exist at all of these lev-els with everyone in their group. The reality is that most people will not get past the social belonging level with their small group. And that is okay. An effective leader will look for connections that she can facilitate with like-minded people in the group. She may never have a personal belonging–level relationship with another member of the group, but she may start the conversation that leads to one between two other people.

We can promise to create environments where intimate commu-nity is possible, but we cannot guarantee that it will happen. Too many groups systems are scored by how many intimate relationships are created, even though most groups never get there. In *Activate*, Nelson Searcy and Kerrick Thomas said it this way:

When we try to induce intimacy, not only do we make it so that people are hesitant to join, we also set up our group leaders for failure. If we set a goal in front of our leaders to get people to enter personal and/or intimate relationships, then they feel like they didn't do their job if everyone in the group doesn't bond and become best friends.[3]

The Perfect Size

We face a constant struggle to define the perfect size of a small group. Too many people in a group, the theory goes, and there will never be room for quiet people to open up. Too few and the group can never gain enough traction to survive.

In his book *David and Goliath*, Malcolm Gladwell takes on the same question when it comes to the perfect classroom size. He points out that the theory that smaller class sizes are more effective is so prevalent that 77 percent of Americans believe it makes more sense to use taxpayer money to lower class size than to raise teachers' salaries. However, studies have proven that smaller class sizes do not necessarily translate into higher test scores. There is a critical mass dynamic that brings out better discussion and engagement from students. Gladwell theorized that the ideal class size is somewhere between eighteen and twenty-four students.[4]

I would argue that there is a similar dynamic when it comes to small groups in a church. The groups who survive the longest and have the most long-term impact tend to be larger. A few benefits of a larger group include these:

- *They are less likely to cancel when a few people are unable to attend a group meeting.* Almost nothing will kill a group faster than group meetings being constantly canceled at the last minute. For a group to survive, it has to be consistent.
- *There is excitement in a room with more people.* When we launch a new service time on Sundays, we know the service is going to survive when it reaches a critical mass. There is anticipation with more people involved.
- *A larger group is able to make a bigger impact through serving.* Instead of just a few people turning out to work on a community project, you have a better chance of attracting a large portion of the group through positive peer pressure.
- *The discussion is richer with a wider array of voices.* More people means more influence from different backgrounds and experiences. A smaller group can be overly influenced by the opinions of the loudest.
- *Larger groups are an easier entry point for outsiders.* It is less intimidating to join a group of fifteen than it is a group of five.

While there are many benefits to starting with a larger group, they also bring their own issues:

- *Having enough space:* The majority of homes cannot comfortably host a really large group.
- *Child care:* The larger the group the more likely they have multiple children.

- *Members not feeling needed:* No one misses them when they don't show up for group.
- *Rabbit trails:* Discussions get routed in too many directions.
- *Anonymity:* It's possible for a group member to attend but never be challenged.

This does not mean that a smaller group cannot be successful. But it does take a different type of leader to help it to survive. You will need to monitor smaller groups more closely to make sure they have the traction to survive.

Sharing the Responsibilities

Almost nothing causes burnout faster with a small-group leader than doing everything for the group himself. Nearly every time I meet with a leader who has requested a break from leading for a season, I find that he was carrying the whole load for his group.

In the Bible, Moses' father-in-law, Jethro, saw that Moses was headed for a crash if he didn't share the burden of leading soon.

The next day Moses took his seat to serve as judge for the people, and they stood around him from morning till evening. When his father-in-law saw all that Moses was doing for the people, he said, "What is this you are doing for the people? Why do you alone sit as judge, while all these people stand around you from morning till evening?"

Moses answered him, "Because the people come to me to seek God's will. Whenever they have a dispute, it is brought to me, and

I decide between the parties and inform them of God's decrees and instructions."

Moses' father-in-law replied, "What you are doing is not good. You and these people who come to you will only wear yourselves out. The work is too heavy for you; you cannot handle it alone." (Exodus 18:13–18, NIV)

Just as with Moses, small-group leaders who are carrying all of the responsibility of leading is not good. They will eventually wear out. Leaders should be trained to delegate tasks such as food preparation, group e-mails, prayer requests, social outings, serving opportunities, and facilitating the discussions. Good leadership is not always about doing the work but rather equipping others to do it with you.

The first step to training leaders to delegate starts with the groups point person modeling it. For the ministry to be effective, we need different voices influencing key decisions. Otherwise it becomes all about us, our goals, our direction, our needs. The apostle Paul admonished church leaders in Ephesians 4:12 "to prepare God's holy people for the work of serving, to make the body of Christ stronger." Too many times we skip the "prepare" part because we believe we can do it better or because we are *paid* to do it.

Preparing doesn't mean just delegating the tasks we don't like to do; it means inviting people who may not necessarily think or act like you to have a voice at the table. Our church and small groups system will be better when we recognize and validate the different gifts of those around us.

With clear expectations and goals that can be easily measured and celebrated, your group leaders and hosts will have the support they need to facilitate healthy groups. Without them, you will constantly be wondering why the best leaders keep dropping out.

Think It Over

- Have you defined what an official small group is at your church? Are they different from ministry teams?
- What are the core elements every successful small group should experience?
- Do you agree that small-group leaders should not teach? Why or why not?
- What are your expectations for curriculum choices in your groups? How many of them are DVD-based teaching?
- What is the ideal size for groups at your church?
- Are you currently clear with your expectations for leaders and hosts? How can you better refine those expectations?

8

Those Questions

Judge a man by his questions
rather than by his answers.
—Voltaire

Part of the process for developing our large-group training every year is surveying our group leaders for their biggest questions about leading or hosting a small group. What is interesting is how most of the questions are the same from year to year. In five years we have changed almost everything about how we approach groups. Sign-ups are different. Curriculum has changed. Training has evolved. But the major questions have not.

I used to believe that a lot of the questions were exclusive to our church and leaders until I started talking to small-groups people around the country. We may design systems completely different with different angles on theology and methodology, but people's needs remain constant. They still need to know how to handle child care for their group.

Because They Asked . . .

What Do We Do About Child Care?

By far the number-one question we get from potential leaders and hosts is about child care. Even if you have a church of entirely twenty-something single adults, they will eventually marry and have kids. We've discovered that the fear of not knowing how to handle child care is the largest barrier for people offering to host a group for the first time.

My wife and I started a young couples group four years ago, partly because we wanted to mentor the next generation through the minefield of young married life, but mostly because we did not want to deal with offering child care. Our small group now has five babies in it, and we are looking at our options for effective child care.

One solution several churches have adopted is offering child care at the church building. This takes the burden off the group leaders for finding babysitters and ensures safety for the kids and peace of mind for the parents. The downside to this solution is it's not scalable as the church grows. Unless you are able to offer child care every night of the week, your groups are forced to meet on the specific days when it is available. This also becomes problematic if your church eventually goes multisite and those satellite campuses are in mobile facilities.

Other churches are successful with offering group leaders a child care stipend or reimbursement to hire babysitters. The church may also offer a list of background-checked child care workers to choose from. But this solution is tough to scale unless your budget can handle exponential growth during the all-church campaigns.

At Cross Point we decided to leave child care solutions up to each group. We address it at the beginning of every semester by giving new leaders and hosts a list of potential options. There are a few of them:

- Each family makes their own arrangements for child care.
- The group pitches in to hire a babysitter to come to the house where the meeting is or to a nearby house. We can offer a list of child care service companies we use occasionally at the church. Each family contributes five to ten dollars per child toward the cost of the sitter.
- Work with the student ministry to hire female babysitters who are raising money for a summer missions trip.
- Work out a co-op relationship with another group that meets on another night.
- Make one night a month a game night where the kids are invited to participate.
- Have one meeting a month where the discussion revolves around the virtue being discussed in our kids ministry and invite the kids to be a part of the discussion that night.

We encourage our groups to allow the kids to participate in group life as much as possible. My kids have always hung out with the group until the discussion time begins and they have to do homework for school. They now look forward to our group meetings more than we do!

Should We Split Our Group?

While splitting or multiplying a group looks great on paper, it is a bad idea in reality. I have never heard someone say, "Our group of friends has gotten too large. Let's split it and you take half of them." That is essentially what we are asking small groups to do when we ask them to multiply into separate groups. We want them to do life together—until they reach a critical mass.

If a group has gotten too large for meaningful discussions, the best option is to subdivide for the discussion time. The group can start together for the meal or hangout time at the beginning, and then come back together for the prayer time at the end. The makeup of the breakout groups can change from week to week based on the topic or stay consistent throughout the semester. This option forces group leaders to develop apprentices who can eventually step out and start new groups for new people.

How Do We Invite Our Neighbors?

If groups are to become the new front door of the church, they have to start with their neighborhood. Our world has changed so that most people don't know their neighbors anymore. When I was growing up, our neighbors were a natural extension of our family. We knew all of our immediate neighbors, and I spent almost as much time in their houses as I did in mine. The thought of inviting a neighbor to your church wasn't that scary at all.

Now, you are lucky to get a cursory wave before the garage door goes down and they disappear into the house. Who has time for connecting with your neighbors anymore? In our first neighborhood when we moved to Nashville, most of the houses had garage entrances on the back of the house. The only way to catch your neighbor was by chasing their car down the driveway and performing a drop-and-roll maneuver under the garage door before it could shut. I couldn't understand why my neighbor wouldn't talk to me again after I did this the first time.

Here are five better ways to connect to your neighbors:

- *Throw a block party.* Everyone needs an excuse to get out and meet the neighbors, so you will be the star for providing one. It's important that this is a no-strings-attached gathering. If neighbors see this party as a pyramid scheme for building your church, you will lose all your equity before it even starts. Opportunities begin as relationships, and block parties set the stage for future friendships.

- *Participate in Halloween.* I understand that not everyone will feel the same way about how to approach this holiday. I don't know another occasion where most of my neighbors will not only be out of their houses at the same time but also spending a few minutes at mine. If you're one of those houses that turns off your lights and hides on Halloween, you're missing a golden opportunity to get to know your neighbors. Also, please don't be the house that puts a gospel tract in the bag with the candy. Be known for having the best candy on the block!

- *Host a movie on your lawn for the families in the neighborhood.* A friend has done this for years and is now the most popular house in the neighborhood. By working at a church, you probably have access to the audio and video equipment to make this a great experience. You can also now affordably rent very large outdoor blow-up screens for your backyard. Put out a few flyers around the neighborhood and fire up the latest Pixar hit.

- *Participate in neighborhood-sponsored events.* Some communities put on an Easter egg hunt or a quarterly "spruce up the 'hood" day. Our neighborhood hosts the largest Oktoberfest in Tennessee every year. More than fifty thousand people descend onto our tiny twelve blocks to eat bratwurst and drink pumpkin-flavored beer. Getting ready for this festival really takes a village.
- *Be the nicest house on the block.* Everyone in the neighborhood knows the houses to avoid approaching. They all know to avoid the people who never acknowledge you when they're walking their dog. Be the complete opposite, and your neighbors will want to get to know you. Offer to loan out your new grill for the neighborhood cookout. Mow the neighbor's lawn occasionally, just because you want to help. All of this creates opportunities for conversations and relationships to begin. The invite to small group or church can come later.

What If No One Shows Up?

It is extremely discouraging to a new group leader or host, who prepares all week for a meeting, to have no one show up. They clean the house, prep for the discussion, buy a few snacks, and no one comes. But it's even worse if just one person shows up.

To keep this from happening, we encourage new groups to take on more people than they can comfortably handle. If they feel like their house can comfortably fit fifteen people, we will open their group to twenty sign-ups because the odds are good that at least five people won't show up.

If a group is struggling to get people signed up at the beginning of a semester, we will look at a few factors to see if it is a viable long-term group:

- *Is the group being hosted in a remote area from the church?* If a leader or host proposes starting a group several miles away from a nucleus of people who attend our church, then we set expectations early that they cannot rely on the church to supply the members for their group. They will need to invite their neighbors and friends or be willing to drive a few minutes to be a part of another group.
- *Is the group's focus too narrow?* Targeting a specific cause for a group to form around can be beneficial, but it will take longer to gain traction. Our women's groups that are focused on the wives of traveling musicians are a good example of this. The first one took a few months to get any momentum, but it meets a huge need in our area.
- *Are they meeting on an unpopular night?* Trying to host a group on Friday nights in a community where high-school football shuts the town down every week is probably going to be a tough go.
- *Are the meetings consistent enough?* Groups that only meet once a month will never gain the relational equity it takes to build loyalty. Even groups who meet every other week will struggle with consistency. If a member

misses one or two meetings in a row, they will be discon-
nected from the life of the group and will probably drop
out. Groups who meet every week have a much higher rate
of success.

- *Is the leader or host too weird?* No matter how amazing the study is, successful groups are formed and grown
through relationships. A leader may have a great heart, but
her awkward personality may be too much of a barrier to
starting a viable group. You may have a few leaders who
need to be encouraged to join other groups.

How Long Should Our Group Meetings Be?

A typical group meeting should take from ninety minutes to two
hours. Groups that meet longer than two hours will limit the type of
people they can keep in the group. Families with young kids will have
bedtime deadlines to keep. Young professionals have early morning
start times to hit.

The most important key to staying on time is setting hard stop
times for group discussions. This will allow group members with
tight schedules to not feel guilty about excusing themselves when
they need to leave, while those who have all the time in the world
can continue to hang out. My small group officially ends at 8:30
p.m., but the last couple usually doesn't leave until around 9:15 p.m.
or later.

How Long Should Our Group Continue to Meet?

Most healthy groups have a life cycle of eighteen to twenty-four
months. After two years of the same group of people meeting together,

their discussions start to feel redundant. The group has a couple of options at this point to get a breath of fresh air:

- They can disband and the leader and an apprentice can start new groups with new people. This is the most effective option for reaching new people in the church with new groups.
- They can integrate new people into the group to bring new voices and personalities into the conversations. It will be difficult, and it will take some time for the new members not to feel like outsiders.

My small group has exercised both options over the past four years. Integrating new people into an existing group has been the most difficult thing for us to do. No matter how inviting or open to new people we are, it still feels like the newcomers are like tenth graders moving to a new school. They don't know the inside jokes. The most successful integration happens when the newcomers already have existing relationships with the group members outside of group meetings and are personally invited to join the group.

How Can We Go Deeper as a Group?

It's pretty easy to lead a group that stays mostly superficial. The conversations around the snacks steer clear of anything beyond sports, kids, and work. The discussions during the study time never get to the openness and confessions that can eventually lead to personal freedom. There is no time spent outside of group meetings in one-on-one life-shaping conversations.

Most small groups resemble an iceberg: 85 percent is below the surface and never seen. To go deeper and discover the rest of the picture takes time and intentionality by the leaders. The quick answer for discovery is strategically choosing the right curriculum, but the study may ask questions that the group may not yet be ready to answer.

The best way to get below the surface of a group is to do a service project together. Gary Smalley suggests that a family that wants to bond should go camping together because something always goes wrong. And when it goes wrong, you gain opportunities to grow closer together as a family.[1]

The same is true for a service project or a short-term mission trip. You will inevitably not have the right kind of supplies and have to get creative. Or it will rain the entire time. Or it takes twice as long as expected, and the group is forced to bond over a common goal of accomplishing the mission. After a group goes through an experience, there will always be "remember when" moments.

A sudden crisis in a group member's life will also bring a group together. A lost loved one, a lost job, a financial crisis, a marriage issue. Shared life experiences will give everyone permission to be vulnerable and to know that we're all in this together.

What Happens When There Is a Breakup Within the Group?

Dealing with the aftermath of a broken relationship within a group can be extremely tricky for a leader. It would be easy for group members to choose sides and splinter the group. The way the leader responds will set the direction of health and reconciliation for the couple and the group. Here are five things a leader should do when this happens:

1. *Do not take sides.* The leader's and members' roles are to love both people unconditionally.

2. *Guide the couple toward professional counseling.* The leader or members should not take on the role of mediator between the couple.

3. *Help them find new groups.* If it's impossible for them to stay in the current group, work with the church leadership to find a group where they can begin to heal.

4. *Be honest and open with the group.* Rumors and speculation will destroy the trust of the group. If there are members who are personally affected by the situation, meet with them individually outside of the normal group meeting time. It might be best to offer to meet with one of the church pastors at this point.

5. *Allow God to strengthen relationships in the group.* Satan wants nothing more than to destroy marriages and relationships, and he will use this opportunity to plant seeds of distrust. Use this time to help couples in the group rededicate themselves to God and to each other. This is an ideal time to take the group through a good marriage study.

Do I Have to Be a Member to Lead a Group?

Each church has a different view when it comes to church membership. For some churches, becoming a member is an essential part of the leadership process. Becoming a member of the church could be a six-step process or a single three-hour class. At Cross Point, we don't make a big deal out of being a member, so we don't require membership before someone can lead or host a small group.

We do ask new leaders to attend a forty-five-minute Discovering Cross Point class.

We also require each group leader to sign an agreement before each semester that allows us to refocus on what the core essentials are as a growing leader. It also gives us a baseline to return to when rare, difficult conversations are needed with a leader. When a leader signs the agreement, he is committing to

- grow within a community of believers radically devoted to Christ, irrevocably committed to one another, and relentlessly dedicated to reaching those outside God's family with the gospel of Christ;
- understand and support the philosophy of ministry, core values, and theology of Cross Point Church;
- facilitate group meetings, pray for group members, and adequately prepare for meetings;
- make the Bible the textbook for all discipleship;
- contact members of the group on a regular basis through e-mail, phone calls, one-on-one meetings, or meeting socially as a group;
- raise up and train apprentice leaders, preparing them for eventual group leadership;
- encourage group members to do an outreach project on a regular basis;
- actively participate in community group leader rallies and one-on-one meetings with their coach or groups director;
- build community among the group by assigning members different roles;

- equip and encourage group members to invite unconnected people into the group;
- cultivate a safe place where true feelings can be shared;
- provide care for group members through prayer, social interaction, and care for special needs. Leaders will notify their coach or groups director of conditions in the group requiring pastoral care and counseling.

It is also extremely important for a group to establish a covenant at the beginning of each semester. The covenant will help the group to avoid unspoken agendas and unmet expectations. With a group covenant, they are committing as a group to

- grow healthy spiritual lives by building a healthy group community;
- give priority to the group meeting and call as soon as possible if they are going to be absent or late;
- create a safe place where people can be heard, feel loved (no quick answers, snapping to judgment, or simple fixes), and know that anything that is shared is confidential and will not be discussed outside the group;
- give the group permission to speak into our lives and help us to live a healthy, balanced spiritual life that is pleasing to God;
- build relationships by getting to know each other and pray for each other regularly;
- invite their friends who might benefit from group and study;
- recognize the importance of helping others experience community by eventually starting a new group.

Because You Asked . . .

A lot of small-group point people have the same questions too. We are all seeking strategies on how to get our pastor more involved in supporting the groups ministry. Or if you have Sunday school, how can it best coexist with off-campus small groups? Or if I can find the money, when, who, and how do I hire for our groups staff team?

What If My Pastor Doesn't Believe in Small Groups?

While it is extremely important for the senior pastor to be an advocate for groups in the church, there may be some work to do to get him there. A church without the pastor as the champion for groups will typically max out at around 40 percent who connect in groups. There are a few things you can do to win him over and reach the other 60 percent and beyond:

- *Bring him stories.* There is no senior pastor who does not get fired up about hearing stories of life change taking place in the church. Send him a monthly e-mail update. Slip them into all-staff meetings. Include him on updates to leaders. If there is a constant flow of life-change stories from the groups team, he will begin to embrace the concept.
- *Show him how key initiatives in the church can be reinforced through small groups.* If there is a building campaign, design a study around it for groups to go through. Or write studies to go along with the weekly messages. Every pastor loves to hear his members still talking about the Sunday message on Wednesday.

- *Allow him to participate in a small group with handpicked members.* Senior pastors feel the pressure to have to lead everything in which they are involved. Give him the opportunity to feel invested in through a group he does not lead. The members of the group should be non-EGRs (extra grace required) people with whom he can be comfortable on a weekly basis.
- *Invite the senior pastor to speak at the next leadership training event.* There is something exhilarating about a roomful of leaders going in the same direction. By participating in the training, he will begin to see the leadership development potential of a well-designed small-group system. Don't forget to fill the night with stories of life change.

Can We Be Successful with Small Groups and Sunday School?

The temptation when building a small-group system in a church with an existing Sunday school system will be to try to kill Sunday school. Not only is this not a good idea but it's not necessary. An effective small-groups system can coexist with Sunday school *if* the objectives and expectations for both are clear.

- What are your Sunday school classes designed to accomplish? Is it biblical knowledge through a lecture format? Or are they building community through discussion? Before you start designing your small groups, solidify what you are already offering through Sunday school classes.

- What percentage of adults is currently in Sunday school? For most churches, that is not going to be 100 percent. A majority of people are not going to participate in a small group and a Sunday school class. If 40 percent of your adult attenders are in Sunday school, 60 percent are still available for off-campus small groups.
- Set clear expectations that small groups are not in competition with Sunday school. Your Sunday school system has probably been around for a while and is working for a percentage of the people. Go out of your way to assure your Sunday school leaders that your goal is to connect the unconnected who would not show up for a Sunday school class.

Once you have established clear expectations and objectives for Sunday school and small groups, there are a few things that can help a launch be successful.

- Invite long-term Sunday school teachers to be a part of the process for building a small-groups system. Dale Carnegie said, "People support a world they help create." There are insights and lessons to learn from someone who has invested their time in discipling others. Animosity can come from a lack of knowledge. Build your first focus group from your most successful Sunday school leaders.
- Start small with a few pilot groups. Instead of launching a huge campaign to take over the church, start with just a couple of groups to ease the church into the concept of off-campus small groups. After those groups have been

running for a while, start sharing with the church the stories coming out of the pilot groups. Use those stories to launch your first large small-group campaign.

- Invite your Sunday school teachers to be a part of your first training sessions. This will help them understand the *why* for off-campus small groups and feel like they are a part of a larger discipleship team. Create a track at your training event just for your Sunday school leaders.

- Celebrate the stories from small groups and Sunday school classes. Ask the Sunday school teachers about spiritual growth and life change happening through the ministry. God doesn't just work in living rooms and kitchens. Celebrate the faithfulness of teachers who are willing to sacrifice each Sunday to show up early and invest in a classroom of adults.

- Design the curriculum for the first all-church study to work in a Sunday-school class format as well as groups.

With extra planning and an inclusive strategy, Sunday school and off-campus small groups can not only coexist but also be an effective two-pronged discipleship strategy.

When and Whom Should We Hire?

A small-groups strategy will only be as successful as the people running it, so it is crucial to make the right choices when it comes time to hire staff. Bill Willits at North Point Church said, "The right person is more important than the system you choose."[2] If you rush into a hiring decision because of a need, it could take years to rebuild the trust lost with the leadership and the church. Start mapping out your metrics early for when a paid position will be needed to adequately care for leaders.

We have found at Cross Point that a volunteer coaching system can adequately care for up to fifty groups. If a part-time position (twenty to thirty hours) is not added at this point, the growth of groups will stall. No matter how high capacity a volunteer staff person is, there is only so much extra time she can give to recruiting and caring for new leaders. A full-time position is needed at around one hundred groups.

A groups director at Cross Point is expected to

- shepherd and equip campus community group leaders through regular one-on-one meetings and large-group training opportunities;
- monitor the health and effectiveness of groups through spiritual health assessments and other tools as needed;
- continually work toward having 100 percent of groups serving in the community through Serving Saturdays and other serving opportunities throughout the year;
- continually recruit new coaches, leaders, and hosts;
- interview and assess new leaders and hosts before the group semester launches;
- help plan and execute three major group launches a year (winter, spring, and fall);
- help plan and execute two leadership rallies a year (January and August);
- help plan and execute two all-church group campaigns a year;
- oversee updating the group data in the church database.

When we are looking to add a paid staff position in our groups department, our first preference is to look within. That is why building our leadership pipeline is so important. We want to tap someone on the shoulder who is already getting it done and understands the DNA of Cross Point. When evaluating a potential candidate, we use Bill Hybels's three Cs[3] and add one to it: character, chemistry, competence, and culture:

- *Character:* Does this person's private life reflect their public image? Are they currently pastoring their family, small group, and other leaders?
- *Chemistry:* Would this person fit in well with the rest of the groups team and staff? Would I be happy to see this person every Monday morning in the office? If this person's caller ID came up on my phone, would I answer it?
- *Competence:* Does this person have a grasp of our strategy for small groups? Do they have the skills and knowledge to help take us to the next level? Are they teachable?
- *Culture:* Cross Point is a unique environment. Will this person have to adjust, or are they already acclimated to how we do ministry? Will the hurdle of adjustment take too long to be effective? Can they handle having Nerf footballs thrown at them at random around the office? Will they throw them back?

Taking your time to make sure a candidate is the right fit for your system will help set your groups up for success. No matter how big the need is, do not rush the process.

Think It Over

- What are the major questions you consistently hear from your small-group leaders?
- Are you answering questions they are not asking in your training?
- Do you currently have an agreement or covenant with your leaders?
- Do you believe that small groups and Sunday school can coexist successfully?
- What is the limit of care for your volunteer leaders?
- What is your process for hiring staff when the time is right?
- What other questions should you be asking right now?

Notes

Introduction

1. *This Emotional Life*, "Connecting," PBS.org, http://www.pbs.org
   /thisemotionallife/topic/connecting/connection-happiness, (accessed
   February 13, 2015). This Emotional Life is a co-production of the
   NOVA/WGBH Science Unity and Vulcan Productions, Inc. A Film
   by Kunhardt McGee Productions. ©/™ 2009 WGBH Educational
   Foundation and Vulcan Productions, Inc. All Rights Reserved.

Chapter 1

1. C. S. Lewis, *The Four Loves* (New York: Houghton Mifflin Harcourt,
   1971), 65.
2. Ted Haggard, *Dog Training, Fly Fishing, and Sharing Christ in the
   21st Century: Empowering Your Church to Build Community Through
   Shared Interests* (Nashville: Thomas Nelson, 2002).
3. See "The 100 Greatest TV Quotes and Catch Phrases," *The NJ Star-
   Ledger*, (Newark, NJ), December 11, 2006.

Chapter 2

1. Susan Cain, *Quiet: The Power of Introverts in a World That Can't Stop
   Talking* (New York: Crown, 2012), 11.
2. Sandra Chambers, "Billy Graham: A Faithful Witness," *Charisma
   News*, November 7, 2013, http://www.charismanews.com/us/41684
   -billy-graham-a-faithful-witness?showall=&start=1, (accessed February
   13, 2015).

Chapter 3

1. Ed Stetzer and Eric Geiger, *Transformational Groups: Creating a New Scorecard for Groups* (Nashville: B&H Publishing Group, 2014), 70.
2. Ibid., 71.
3. Andy Stanley, Session One at the 2013 re:group Conference in Atlanta, Georgia.
4. "Adopt-a-Block," DreamCenter.org, http://www.dreamcenter.org/community-outreach/adopt-a-block/, (accessed February 9, 2015).
5. "Starting Point: A 10-Week Small Group Conversation about the Story of God," StartingPoint.com, http://startingpoint.com/, (accessed February 9, 2015).

Chapter 4

1. Andy Stanley, Session One at the 2009 Catalyst Conference in Atlanta, Georgia.

Chapter 5

1. Dave Ferguson and Jon Ferguson, *Exponential: How You and Your Friends Can Start a Missional Church Movement* (Grand Rapids: Zondervan, 2010).
2. John C. Maxwell, *The Five Levels of Leadership: Proven Steps to Maximize Your Potential* (New York: Center Street, 2011).
3. Geoff Surratt, Greg Ligon, and Warren Bird, *The Multi-Site Church Revolution: Being One Church—in Many Locations* (Grand Rapids: Zondervan, 2006), 150–51. Used by permission of Zondervan. www.zondervan.com.

Chapter 6

1. Bob Goff, *Love Does: Discover a Secretly Incredible Life in an Ordinary World* (Nashville: Thomas Nelson, 2012).
2. "The Chicken Roaster," *Seinfeld*, Season 8, Episode 8, (November 14, 1996), http://www.seinfeldscripts.com/TheChickenRoaster.htm, (accessed February 9, 2015).

3. Simon Sinek, "How Great Leaders Inspire Action," (September 2009), http://www.ted.com/talks/simon_sinek_how_great_leaders_inspire_action?language=en, (accessed February 9, 2015).

Chapter 7
1. Rick Howerton, *A Different Kind of Tribe: Embracing the New Small-Group Dynamic* (Colorado Springs: NavPress, 2012), 78.
2. Joseph R. Myers, *Organic Community: Creating a Place Where People Naturally Connect* (Grand Rapids: Baker, 2007).
3. Nelson Searcy and Kerrick Thomas, *Activate: An Entirely New Approach to Small Groups* (Ventura, CA: Regal, 2008), 25.
4. Malcolm Gladwell, "Chapter Two: Teresa DeBrito," in *David and Goliath: Underdogs, Misfits, and the Art of Battling Giants* (New York: Little Brown and Company, 2013).

Chapter 8
1. Gary Smalley, *Love is a Decision* (Nashville: Word, 1989), 152–172.
2. Bill Willits, Proceedings of Group 100 Conference, Lifeway Christian Resources, Nashville, 2014.
3. Bill Hybels, *Courageous Leadership* (Grand Rapids: Zondervan, 2002), 81.

About the Author

Chris Surratt is a ministry consultant and coach with over twenty-two years of experience serving the local church. Most recently, Chris was the Pastor of Adult Ministries at Cross Point Church in Nashville, Tennessee, where he oversaw and helped guide small groups and global and local good across five campuses.

Before coming to Cross Point in 2009, Chris was on staff at Seacoast Church in Charleston, South Carolina, for fifteen years, serving as a worship arts pastor, campus pastor and on the directional leadership team. Both Cross Point and Seacoast have been recognized as two of the fastest growing churches in the United States.

Chris also works with Leadership Network in creating collaborative learning environments for churches across the world. He is passionate about helping people find their next steps toward God within the context of community.

You can find Chris blogging regularly at www.chrissurratt.com on the subjects of community, discipleship, and leadership. Chris enjoys exploring and living in downtown Nashville with his wife and two daughters.

ALSO AVAILABLE FROM

NE⧓T

LEADERSHIP NETWORK

WHEREVER BOOKS ARE SOLD

ISBN: 9780718031190
ISBN: 9780718031206 (E-BOOK)